Timothy Hopkins

Sherwood Hall Nursery Co. materials

Timothy Hopkins

Sherwood Hall Nursery Co. materials

ISBN/EAN: 9783741138782

Manufactured in Europe, USA, Canada, Australia, Japa

Cover: Foto ©Thomas Meinert / pixelio.de

Manufactured and distributed by brebook publishing software
(www.brebook.com)

Timothy Hopkins

Sherwood Hall Nursery Co. materials

1893

—Catalogue—

2797

Sherwood Hall Nursery Co.

—Timothy Hopkins—

Exporters · Importers and Growers of

Trees · Plants · Seeds · Bulbs

427-429 Sansome St.
and 501-503 Clay St.

San Francisco, California

→ Nurseries, Menlo Park ←

SHERWOOD HALL NURSERY CO.'S

POPULAR COLLECTIONS OF SEEDS PLANTS AND BULBS.

Special attention is invited to this page, the following Collections being of excellent value. In most cases, if selected at regular catalogue rates, they would cost one-third more than they are now offered for. Each Collection contains only the most desirable varieties in its class, and many of our customers who have not time to make a selection will realize that this is a convenient mode of ordering. No reduction in the price of these Collections can be made, and in view of the large value for the money, we can make no change in the assortments; they are put up in large quantities in advance of our busy season.

COLLECTIONS OF FLOWER SEEDS FREE BY MAIL.

The following Collections contain the most showy varieties in our large assortment, with full directions for culture. Each packet contains a mixture of the different colors of its species, so that a greater display can be made at less cost than when ordered in separate packets.

Collection of 10 Choice Varieties of Ornamental Foliage Plants $0.50
Collection of 12 Choice Varieties of Annuals 50
Collection of 20 Choice Varieties suitable for Bouquets . .75
Collection of 8 Distinct Colors of Double Hollyhocks . .75
Collection of 12 Distinct Colors of Large-flowered Pansy 1.00
Collection of 21 Distinct Colors Sweet Peas (see illustrations on back cover) 1.50

☞ Any one remitting $4.50 will receive the above six superb collections free by mail.

COMPLETE ASSORTMENTS OF VEGETABLE SEEDS.

These Collections can be sent by mail, but will carry in much better shape if sent by express.	No. 1, $5. *If by mail, add $1.25 for postage.*	No. 2, $10. *If by mail, add $2 for postage.*	No. 3, $15. *If by mail, add $3 for postage.*	No. 4, $20. *If by mail, add $4 for postage.*
Beans. Green-podded, wax and pole varieties	5 lbs.	10 lbs.	12 lbs.	15 lbs.
Beets. Best table sorts	3 ozs.	½ lb.	¾ lb.	1 lb.
Broccoli. Mammoth White	pkt.	pkt.	¼ oz.	½ oz.
Brussels Sprouts. Improved Dwarf	pkt.	½ oz.	1 oz.	2 ozs.
Cabbage. Best early and late varieties	1 oz.	3 ozs.	4 ozs.	6 ozs.
Carrots. Best table sorts	2 ozs.	4 ozs.	6 ozs.	8 ozs.
Cauliflower. Early and late varieties	2 pkts.	¼ oz.	½ oz.	1 oz.
Celery. Perfection, Hartwell and White Plume	½ oz.	¾ oz.	1 oz.	2 ozs.
Corn. Early, medium and late sugar varieties	2 lbs.	4 lbs.	5 lbs.	6 lbs.
Corn Salad. Large-leaved	pkt.	½ oz.	1 oz.	2 ozs.
Cress, or Pepper Grass	1 oz.	2 ozs.	¼ lb.	½ lb.
Cucumber. The most desirable varieties	1 oz.	2 ozs.	3 ozs.	¼ lb.
Egg Plant. Improved New York Purple	pkt.	¼ oz.	½ oz.	1 oz.
Endive. Green-curled	½ oz.	1 oz.	2 ozs.	3 ozs.
Kale. Dwarf Green-curled	pkt.	½ oz.	1 oz.	2 ozs.
Kohlrabi. Early White Vienna	pkt.	½ oz.	1 oz.	2 ozs.
Leek. Large London Flag	pkt.	½ oz.	1 oz.	2 ozs.
Lettuce. Curled, Cabbage and Cos varieties	1 oz.	3 ozs.	4 ozs.	5 ozs.
Melons, Musk and Water. Best varieties	4 pkts.	¼ lb.	½ lb.	¾ lb.
Okra. Dwarf Density	1 oz.	2 ozs.	¼ lb.	½ lb.
Onion. American, Bermuda and Italian sorts	2 ozs.	¼ lb.	½ lb.	1 lb.
Parsley. Extra Double-curled	½ oz.	1 oz.	2 ozs.	¼ lb.
Parsnip. Improved Hollow-crown	1 oz.	2 ozs.	¼ lb.	½ lb.
Peas. Best varieties for succession of crops	5 lbs.	10 lbs.	15 lbs.	20 lbs.
Pepper. The most popular kinds	pkt.	¼ oz.	½ oz.	1 oz.
Radish. The recent Improved French varieties	3 ozs.	6 ozs.	½ lb.	¾ lb.
Salsify. Mammoth Sandwich Island	1 oz.	2 ozs.	¼ lb.	½ lb.
Spinach. Long-standing	¼ lb.	½ lb.	¾ lb.	1 lb.
Squash. Summer and winter sorts	1 oz.	2 ozs.	4 ozs.	6 ozs.
Tomato. All favorite varieties	4 pkts.	2 ozs.	3 ozs.	¼ lb.
Turnip. Early and late table sorts	2 ozs.	4 ozs.	6 ozs.	¾ lb.
Herbs. Five leading kinds	3 pkts.	5 pkts.	5 pkts.	5 pkts.

$

DOLLAR COLLECTIONS OF PLANTS AND BULBS FREE BY MAIL.

The following collections of plants and bulbs, all distinctly labeled, will be forwarded free, by mail, to any post office in the United States or Canada. We send only strong, healthy plants, securely packed, which is a guarantee of success.

Carnations Portia, Silver Spray, Lizzie McGowan, Indiana, Day-Break, Annie Wiegand, American Flag, Black Knight, American Wonder, Puritan, Cherry Lips, Fred Dorner.

Twelve Healthy Pot-grown Plants of the above Varieties for ONE DOLLAR.

Chrysanthemums Ada Spaulding, Domination, Louis Boehmer, Mrs. Langtry, John Thorpe, Adirondack, Henry Turner, Frank Thomson, Pelican, Cullingfordii, Mrs. Carnegie, Henry Connell.

Twelve Healthy Pot-grown Plants of the above Varieties for ONE DOLLAR.

Pelargoniums Beauty of Oxton, Dr. Masters, Duchess of Bedford, Empress of India, Glorie de Tours, Kingston Beauty, Mrs. John Saul, Mme. Thibaut, Golden Gate, David Nully, Mme. Everard, Mrs. Coupland.

Twelve Healthy Pot-grown Plants of the above Varieties for ONE DOLLAR.

Roses Catharine Mermet, Perle des Jardins, Papa Gontier, Niphetos, The Bride, La France, Climbing Niphetos, Duchess of Albany, Waban, Rainbow, American Beauty, Gen. Jacqueminot.

Twelve Healthy Pot-grown Plants of the above Varieties for ONE DOLLAR.

Forty Flowering Bulbs One each, Lilium Auratum, Lilium Longiflorum, Calla Lily, Cyclamen, Tuberose. Two each, Lilium Humboldtii, Montbretia, Anemones, Ranunculus, Star of Bethlehem, Madeira Vine, Gladiolus. Three each, Mariposa Lily, Milla Biflora, Bessera Elegans, Oxalis Decaphylla, Zephyranthes Rosea, and six Freesia Refracta Alba. **Forty Strong Flowering Bulbs, as above mentioned, for ONE DOLLAR.**

☞ The foregoing collections are subject to slight variation, as some of the stock may become exhausted towards the end of the season, and unless advised to the contrary, we will take the liberty to substitute other as good or better varieties; in every case, however, the full forty bulbs and plants will be sent.

ORDER SHEET.

TREES, PLANTS, SEEDS, BULBS.

SHERWOOD HALL NURSERY CO., SAN FRANCISCO, CAL.

POSTAGE.—If purchasers desire their orders forwarded by mail, add to catalogue prices, for postage, at the rate of eight cents per pound, when ordering in quantities of half-pound and upwards. We prepay postage when the order is for ounces and packets. In cases where postage is not allowed, we shall deduct a sufficient quantity to cover deficiency, to avoid the necessity of opening accounts for small balances.

We believe our stock is as represented; but at the same time wish to be distinctly understood that our seeds are sold without any warranty, express or implied, and without any responsibility in respect to the crop. If our seeds are not accepted on these terms, they must be returned at once.

☞ Special prices to market gardeners and public institutions using large quantities of seeds.

VERY IMPORTANT.—Write your name very plainly in black ink, and give your Post Office, County and State in full every time.

Your Name _____ Very plain.

Post Office _____

County _____

State _____

Express Office { If different } from P. O.

Forward by { Mail, Express } or Freight.

AMOUNT ENCLOSED.

No Goods Sent C. O. D.

Money Order,	$
Draft,	$
Stamps,	$
Postal Notes,	$
Cash,	$
Date,	189

Please do not write here.

No.	Qts.	Pints.	Lbs.	Ozs.	Pkts.	Number Planter Bulbs.	NAMES OF ARTICLES WANTED.	PRICE.

NAMES	P. O.	STATE	NAMES	P. O.	STATE

We will consider it a special favor if you write below the names of some of your friends who are likely to use Trees, Plants, Seeds, Bulbs.

A Little Introductory Talk.

THE Sherwood Hall Nursery Company have pleasure in presenting with their compliments their first General Catalogue of everything pertaining to horticultural and kindred pursuits ; for although they have succeeded in gaining a desirable reputation in the sale of trees and plants in past years, this is their first presentation of a complete general assortment, including the best current varieties of seeds and bulbs.

We have endeavored to make our Catalogue complete and convenient, and will be thankful for suggestions or opinions that may be utilized in coming issues. It is proper to here mention our facilities for serving you : We have large establishments in operation, including a depot in San Francisco, where Trees, Plants, Seeds and Bulbs of every description can be obtained, and extensive greenhouses and nurseries at Menlo Park (30 miles from San Francisco), providing exceptional facilities for growing and testing stock in the most careful manner. Visitors are always welcome at our Menlo Park place, and a day can be profitably spent in looking over our greenhouses and grounds, which are extensive and attractively situated. Both of these establishments are admittedly a credit to California, and compare favorably with similar interests anywhere in the country. Planters on the Pacific coast are asked to notice that they have now an opportunity to purchase all garden supplies under favorable circumstances near at hand, saving thus both time and expense, and fostering a home enterprise. Our field will embrace the limitless flora of the Pacific Coast and Japan, supplemented by whatever the rest of the world can supply, as dictated by the educated taste of our patrons.

Although comparatively young in the trade, our establishment is equipped with facilities and stock for transacting a large volume of business. There is nothing experimental in dealing with us, and our financial resources enable us to buy in such a manner as to quote our patrons favorable prices. MR. JAMES B. KIDD, recently with Messrs. James M. Thorburn & Co., of New York, has charge of our seed and bulb departments, and in each branch of our business we have skilled assistants.

An effort has been made to render the pages of this Catalogue not only descriptive but agreeably instructive, and we trust our friends may find herein aids to success in the garden.

How to do Business with Us.

It costs nothing additional to order early, and you thus secure first choice and best attention.

Don't forget to write your name and address, postoffice, express office and state on every order. Give plain shipping directions, and state whether you wish your order sent by freight, express or mail. When this is omitted we use our best judgment, and are not responsible should it prove unsatisfactory to you.

It is important to send cash with orders, as we do not open accounts for small amounts. Remit by registered letter, money order, or if small amounts, postage stamps will do.

We are determined to do business so as to give our customers entire satisfaction, and by equitable transactions to secure their permanent trade and a word of recommendation to their neighbors and friends. We do not claim to sell the cheapest seeds or plants, but the BEST, and know that if favored with a share of your orders for the coming season our goods will give you satisfaction. We believe our stock is as represented ; but at the same time wish to be distinctly understood that our seeds are sold without any warranty, express or implied, and without any responsibility in respect to the crop. If our seeds are not accepted on these terms, they must be returned at once.

Sherwood Hall Nursery Co.

Timothy Hopkins.

Greenhouses, Nursery and Seed Farms, Menlo Park, California.   427-429 Sansome Street) 501-503 Clay Street) San Francisco, California.

A Handsome Lawn: How to Have It.

WHAT IS more attractive than a home surrounded by a well-kept, velvet-like lawn? But just how to produce it is more or less of a mystery to some. An essential condition in making such a lawn as you would like to have is, that the ground be thoroughly cleansed of all root-weeds before sowing. It should be dug or trenched to an equal depth and repeatedly trodden, rolled and leveled, until at last a firm, uniform surface is obtained. The selection of proper grass-seeds is the important matter, and this requires more than ordinary attention, so that the kinds of grass be suited both to the purpose and soil, and that the mixture of these grasses be proportioned to the end in view. It must be remembered that much of the fine appearance of a lawn depends upon regularity in mowing, as, if left too long before this operation is commenced, or if, when well established, it is not closely mown, the stronger grasses will overgrow the weaker, thus destroying smoothness of surface, till ultimately the whole becomes patchy and unsightly. The seed may be sown in spring or fall, but if sown in hot weather a slight sowing of oats with the grass will serve to protect the delicate growth. For forming new lawns fifty or sixty pounds of seed are required per acre, and for the renovation of old ones half that quantity will give good results.

MENLO PARK LAWN GRASS. We devote great care to the preparation of this article, and by careful tests have proved its superiority over all other mixtures. It is composed of the very choicest selected fancy cleaned grasses, entirely free from seeds of weeds, and we can with confidence recommend it to those who wish their lawns to present an evergreen, carpet-like appearance. Price per pound, 30 cents. For the convenience of those who require only a small quantity of seed, MENLO PARK LAWN GRASS is put up in boxes containing sufficient for 300 square feet. We forward these boxes, free by mail, at 25 cents each.

Lawn-Grass Mixture. This is the mixture usually sold by other seedsmen, and being less expensive than the foregoing, may be suitable where a high degree of elegance is not demanded. Price per pound, 25 cents.

Lawn Fertilizer. Unless thoroughly decomposed, stable-manure is not desirable, because of the number of weed-seeds contained in it. Our Lawn Fertilizer possesses the requisite properties to induce a rapid, luxuriant growth, and should be sown broadcast at the rate of 1,500 pounds per acre. A 10-pound package is sufficient for 300 square feet. Price per ton, $45; per 10-pound package, 75 cents.

Rubber Hose, "Maltese Cross" Brand. This is the best rubber hose in the market, made from pure Para rubber and Sea Island duck. Both duck and rubber are charged with carbolic acid, which prevents mildew and rot. Price per foot:

	⅝-in.	¾-in.	1-in.	1¼-in.	1½-in.
3-ply	$0.18½	.22	.28	.35	.42
4-ply	$0.21	.29	.35	.42	.53

Prices of larger sizes on application.

Rubber Hose, "Wallabout" Brand. Warranted of fine material and superior workmanship, and is the best medium-priced hose ever produced. Price per foot:

	⅝-in.	¾-in.	1-in.	1¼-in.	1½-in.
3-ply	$0.10	.13	.18	.23	.27
4-ply	$0.13	.17	.22	.28	.34

Prices of larger sizes on application.

Hose-Menders. Superior to any other in the market, both for durability and ease of adjustment. In three sizes: ½-in., 50 cents per dozen; ¾-in., 60 cents per dozen; 1-in., $1.25 per dozen. Single ones of either size, 10 cents each.

Selected Seeds.

NEW AND STANDARD VEGETABLES,

Embracing all the best varieties in cultivation, with directions for their culture.

IMPORTANT.—Market-gardeners, public institutions and clubs who use seeds in large quantities will save money by writing us for special quotations. It is no trouble to give estimates or information.

POSTAGE.—*If purchasers desire their orders forwarded by mail, add to catalogue prices, for postage, at the rate of eight cents per pound, when ordering in quantities of half-pound and upwards. We prepay postage when the order is for ounces and packets. In cases where postage is not allowed, we shall deduct a sufficient quantity to cover deficiency, to avoid the necessity of opening accounts for small balances.*

Artichoke.

French, *Artichaut.* German, *Artichoke.* Spanish, *Alcachofa.*

CULTURE.—One ounce will produce five hundred plants. Sow in drills one foot apart and two inches deep, in moist, rich soil, and transplant to permanent beds, allowing a space of three feet between the rows and four feet between each plant. Liberal treatment will insure those fine heads so greatly prized.

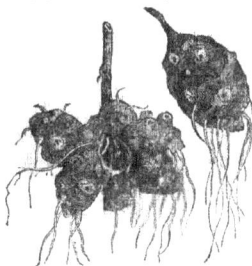

JERUSALEM ARTICHOKE.

	Oz.	¼-lb.	Lb.
Large Green Globe. The best for general cultivation	$0 30	$0 90	$3 00
Strong, two-year-old roots of this variety . . . . per doz., $2 .			
Jerusalem Artichoke. (*Helianthus tuberosus.*) Not produced from seed; very productive, the yield often exceeding one thousand bushels per acre. Valuable for stock feeding . . per 100 lbs., $15 .			20

Asparagus.

French, *Asberge.* German, *Spargel.* Spanish, *Esparrago.*

CULTURE.—One ounce will produce six hundred plants, and sow sixty feet of drill. Beds are usually formed by setting out two or three-year-old roots, but if you wish to raise from seed, sow in drills eighteen inches apart and one and a-half inches deep; thin early, leaving fifteen inches between the plants. At one or two years old transplant to permanent beds, well manured and thoroughly trenched to the depth of two feet. Set the plants in rows three to four feet apart and two feet distant in the rows, carefully spreading out the roots and covering from six to eight inches. Every fall apply a good dressing of thoroughly decomposed manure, and in spring fork this in thoroughly. A dressing of coarse salt, given once a year at the rate of two pounds to the square yard, will be beneficial. Cutting may commence the third year from sowing.

	Oz.	¼-lb.	Lb.
Conover's Colossal. A large, early variety; the best for general use	$0 10	$0 25	$0 60
Two-year old roots . . . . per 100, $2; per 1,000, $10 .			
Palmetto. A recent introduction; more productive than the preceding, and of a bright green color	10	30	9?
Two-year old roots . . . . per 100, $2.25; per 1,000, $12.50 .			

If roots are ordered by mail, add 50 cents per hundred for postage.

All packets in this Catalogue are 5 cents, except where noted.

Beans.
DWARF SNAP or BUSH.

French, *Haricot Nain.* German, *Busch-bohnen.* Spanish, *Frijole Nano.*

☞ *Under this head are classed all the low-growing sorts, variously called Bush, Snap, String, Wax or French Beans.*

CULTURE.—One pound will sow one hundred feet of drill; one hundred pounds is required for an acre. A light, rich soil is best. Plant the seeds two inches deep and three inches apart, in rows two feet apart. When the plants are three inches high, and again when about to flower, draw the earth carefully up around the stems. Keep well cultivated, as no crop better repays extra labor in this direction.

There has been a vast improvement in these Dwarf Beans of late years, and the varieties now offered leave little to be desired. With good culture they are very profitable for market.

	Pkt.	Lb.	100 lbs.
Best of All. Wonderfully productive, early and tender	$0 10	$0 15	$10 00
Black-Eyed Wax. Distinct and valuable variety; very robust, early and productive	10	15	8 50
Black Wax. A well-known standard sort, still very popular	$0 10	$0 13	$8 00
Canadian Wonder. Handsome flat pods of great length; tender and of fine flavor	10	20	12 00
Crystal Wax. Pods of fair size, very tender, stringless and productive	10	15	10 00
Dwarf Horticultural. A bush variety of the well-known Horticultural Pole Bean	10	15	12 00
Dwarf Lima (Henderson's). A variety of great merit, one of its most valuable characteristics being extreme earliness, while for quality and productiveness this delicious vegetable has no rival	10	20	12 00
Early China. A well-known sort, desirable on account of earliness	10	12	7 50
Extra Early Refugee. A recent introduction, fast becoming indispensable on account of its earliness and productiveness	10	17	12 50
Extra Early Valentine. Differing from the ordinary Red Valentine only in earliness; usually ready for table in forty days from time of planting	10	15	8 50
Improved Golden Wax. A vigorous grower, enormously productive and of grand quality; a great improvement on the old variety	10	13	9 00
Long Yellow Six-Weeks. A standard sort for market or family use	10	12	8 00
Low's Champion. Produces an abundance of stringless, fleshy, flat pods containing five to seven beans of excellent flavor, either green or dry	10	15	10 00
Mohawk. A hardy early variety, largely grown for market use	10	13	9 00
Refugee or Thousand-to-One. A standard sort for general crop; very prolific	10	12	7 50
Wardwell's Kidney Wax. The perfection of Wax Beans, being extra early, prolific, handsome and free from rust	10	15	10 00
White Kidney. One of the best for shelling, either dry or green	10	12	7 50
White Marrow. An old favorite, similar to the preceding	10	12	7 50
White Wax. Similar to Black Wax except in color of seed	10	13	8 00

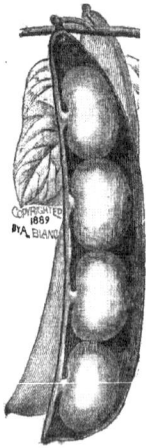

HENDERSON'S DWARF LIMA.

Don't forget that postage on Beans is 8 cents per pound.

BEANS, ENGLISH.

French, *Feve de Marais.* German, *Grosse Bohnen.* Spanish, *Haba.*

CULTURE.—One pound will sow fifty feet of drill. Select a warm situation, and plant two inches deep in double rows, allowing four inches between the two lines forming the row and three feet between the double rows. Pinch out the top when the bloom shows strong, and keep the ground well cultivated and clean.

	Pkt.	Lb.	100 lbs.
Broad Windsor. Superior to all other types of this class of Beans	$0 10	$0 15	$8 50
Early Mazagen. Smaller than the preceding; hardy and productive	10	15	8 00

BEANS, POLE or RUNNING.

French, *Haricots a Rames.* German, *Stangen Bohnen.* Spanish, *Frijole Vastago.*

CULTURE.—One pound will plant fifty hills; thirty pounds will plant an acre. The soil should be mellow, rich and warm. Lay the ground out in hills four feet apart each way, and set poles eight or ten feet long firmly in the hills before putting in the seed. Plant five or six beans in a hill, and cover about two inches deep; leave three healthy plants at each pole, and when a few inches high draw a little earth around them as support. Use the cultivator freely to keep the soil mellow and clean.

	Pkt.	Lb.	100 lbs.
Dreer's Lima. Smaller beans, but earlier and more prolific than Large Lima	$0 10	$0 20	$15 00
Dutch Case-Knife. An old-fashioned productive and early variety	10	15	12 00
Extra Early Jersey Lima. Fully two weeks earlier than any other Pole Lima; they are always tender and delicious	10	25	18 00
Golden Cluster. Produces long, golden yellow, stringless pods, tender and of delicious quality	10	25	20 00
Horticultural or Speckled Cranberry. Popular old favorite; useful either green or dried	10	15	12 00
Large White Lima. Always popular, and only surpassed by other sorts in earliness	10	15	10 00
Scarlet Runners. Ornamental and useful; produces brilliant scarlet flowers, and the beans are used either green or shelled	10	20	15 00
Yard Long or Cuban Asparagus. Produces pods of extraordinary length, sometimes over two feet, and so abundantly as almost to conceal the foliage of the vine	15	50	

Broccoli.

French, *Chou Brocoli.* German, *Spargel-Kohl.* Spanish, *Brocoli.*

CULTURE.—One ounce will produce three thousand plants. Sow thinly in seed beds. For permanent location select fresh land, deeply tilled. When the plants are strong enough set out in rows two feet apart each way, putting the plants well down to their lower leaves. Cultivate frequently the ground between the rows, and give a plentiful supply of water during all stages of their growth.

	Oz.	¼-lb.	Lb.
Christmas White. Dwarf, compact habit; firm white heads of fine quality	$0 60	$2 00	$7 00
Improved Purple Cape. A standard sort, very hardy and productive	30	80	3 00
Walcheren. Produces large white heads of superior quality; very popular, and sells well wherever offered to the public	40	1 25	4 00

What do you think of the last page of the cover?

Beet and Mangel-Wurzel.

French, *Betterave.* German, *Runkelrüben.* Spanish, *Remolacha.*

CULTURE.—One ounce will sow fifty feet of drill; five pounds will sow an acre. Rich, deep soil not too recently manured is best for this crop; sow about two inches deep in drills fifteen inches apart, and when well established thin the plants to six inches apart in the rows. Mangel-Wurzels should be planted in rows two feet apart, and thinned to eight inches in the rows. To obtain the best results from this crop, deep soil, well plowed, and a liberal application of an honest chemical fertilizer are necessary.

	Oz.	¼-lb.	1.b.
Dewing's Extra Early Turnip. Flesh deep blood-red, tender and sweet . . .	$0 10	$0 25	$0 75
Early Bassano. Very early; flesh pink, zoned with white; sweet and tender when young	10	25	75
Early Blood Turnip. Dark red, tender, and keeps well	10	20	60
Eclipse. Extra early, uniform shape, bright red, fine grained and delicious	10	25	75
Edmand's. Handsome shape; flesh of a dark blood-red, sweet and tender	10	25	75
Egyptian Blood Turnip. Well-known variety, of a rich, deep crimson color . .	10	20	60
Long Smooth Blood. An excellent large, late variety	10	20	60
Swiss Chard. Known also as *Silver* or *Sea Kale Beet.* Cultivated only for its leaves, the mid-ribs of which are cooked like Asparagus	10	25	75

ECLIPSE BEET.

FIELD BEETS.

	Oz.	¼-lb.	Lb.
French White Sugar Beet. Grows to a large size; exceedingly rich in sugar	$0 10	$0 15	$0 50
Golden Tankard Mangel-Wurzel. Nutritious, and valued for its milk-producing qualities	10	15	50
Mammoth Long Red Mangel-Wurzel. This variety grows to an immense size, and is the most desirable sort to grow for stock-feeding. (See cut to the right.)	40	15	50
Orange Globe. Useful in shallow ground; productive and a good keeper	10	15	40
Red Globe. Similar to the preceding, except in color . . .	10	15	40

Brussels Sprouts.

French, *Chou de Bruxelles.* German, *Rosenkohl.* Spanish, *Berza de Bruseis.*

CULTURE.—One ounce will produce three thousand plants. Sow as directed for Broccoli, and set the plants in permanent quarters two and a-half feet apart each way. They require a long season of growth, but with suitable soil and liberal manuring an excellent crop of this most delicious vegetable can be secured. The splendid flavor of properly cooked Brussels Sprouts would commend them to epicures and others if generally known. Though of the cabbage family, the flavor is far more delicate and pleasing than that of any cabbage. This vegetable is one of the old world's productions which has yet to become thoroughly well known in the new world, and when it does, it will be as popular here as it is elsewhere.

	Oz.	¼-lb.	1 b
Improved Dwarf. Very productive, tender and of rich flavor	$0 20	$0 60	$2 00
Matchless. Of vigorous growth, productive and of delicious flavor	25	75	2 50

BRUSSELS SPROUTS.

MAMMOTH LONG RED MANGEL WURZEL.

A trial will convince that QUALITY is our Motto.

Cabbage.

French, *Chou Pomme.* German, *Kopf-Kohl.* Spanish, *Col repollo.*

CULTURE.—One ounce will produce three thousand plants; five ounces will produce sufficient plants for an acre. Although Cabbage can be grown on any richly manured soil, a deep, mellow loam inclining to clay is to be preferred. Set the plants in rows fifteen to thirty inches apart, the distance between the rows generally being two feet, but varying according to the variety of Cabbage, the small early sorts requiring a lesser distance than the large late varieties. When setting out, be particular that the plants are placed down to the first leaf, so that all the stem is under ground. Use the cultivator or hoe frequently, stirring the ground deeper as they advance in growth, and drawing up a little earth to the plants each time. Should the cabbage-worm or other insect pests annoy, "Hammond's Slug Shot" is safe, easily applied and effectual; do not delay in thus removing any insects that may appear.

Earliest.

	Oz.	¼-lb.	Lb.
Earliest Etampes. Very early, medium-sized, heart-shaped heads	$0 20	$1 50	$1 50
Early French Oxheart. Solid, conical-shaped heads of good size	25	60	2 00
Early York. A small, early-heading, popular variety	15	40	1 25
Large Early York. Larger than the preceding, and a few days later	15	40	1 25

Medium.

	Oz.	¼-lb.	Lb.
All-Seasons. Most desirable in this section; heads of good size and quality; one of the best varieties yet introduced	25	75	2 50
Fliderkraut. A favorite German sort; conical heads, with few outside leaves	20	50	1 50
Fottler's Brunswick. The earliest of this type; a sure header and very popular	25	75	2 50
Improved Summer. Probably the best large early; uniform and of large size, heads frequently weighing twelve to fifteen pounds	30	80	3 00
Selected Jersey Wakefield. This strain is not so pointed as the ordinary Wakefield, but is equally as early and a more reliable header	30	80	3 00
Succession. A recent introduction of great merit; a valuable market-garden sort	40	1 00	3 50
Winnigstadt. Medium to large conical shaped heads, very solid; an old and entirely reliable variety which has not been supplanted in public favor	25	75	2 50

Late.

	Oz.	¼-lb.	Lb.
Large Late Drumhead. An old favorite, with broad, flat, compact heads	20	50	1 50
Marblehead Mammoth. A coarse-growing variety of enormous size	15	40	1 25
Premium Flat Dutch. Selected strain of immense size, and without doubt the most sure header we know of; tender, crisp and of delicious flavor	30	80	3 00
Stone-Mason. A small, solid, flat head, sweet and tender	25	75	2 50

Red.

	Oz.	¼-lb.	Lb.
Erfurt Early Blood Red. Extra early, deep blood red; excellent for pickling	20	50	1 50
Mammoth Red Rock. A late, very large, solid, fine strain	40	1 25	4 00

Savoy.

	Oz.	¼-lb.	Lb.
American Drumhead. A splendid strain, producing very large solid heads of a rich, dark green color	30	80	3 00
Early Dwarf Ulm. Very early, small round heads of first-rate quality	20	50	1 50
Green Globe. Good, solid heads, finely curled and very hardy	15	40	1 25

Johnson Grass is the best Forage Plant grown.

Carrot.

French, *Carotte.* German, *Möhren.* Spanish, *Zanahoria.*

CULTURE.—One ounce will sow one hundred and fifty feet of drill; three pounds are required for an acre. The most suitable soil is a rich, deep, sandy loam, not too recently manured. Sow rather thinly in drills twelve to fifteen inches apart, according to the sorts, thinning out to six or seven inches between the plants. In field culture the rows should be all of two feet apart, so that the crop can be worked with the horse cultivator.

GUERANDE OR OXHEART.

	Oz.	¼-lb.	Lb.
Altringham. Similar to Large Orange; mild and well-flavored	$0 10	$0 20	$0 50
Bellot. Very early and tender; excellent for forcing	15	40	1 50
Danvers Half-Long. Of good quality and exceedingly productive	10	25	75
Earliest French Forcing. Roots small, globe-shaped; delicious flavor; the very best early	10	30	1 00
Early Scarlet Horn. Deep red flesh, tender and delicate	10	25	75
Guerande or Oxheart. Thick and short; of fine color and flavor	10	30	1 00
Half-Long Stump-Rooted. Smooth and handsome; a popular favorite	10	25	75

Improved Long Orange. A careful selection; bright orange-red; excellent for main crop . . . . Oz. $0 10   ¼-lb. $0 25   Lb. $0 75

Long White Belgian. A productive variety for field culture 10   20   50

DANVERS HALF-LONG CARROT.

Cauliflower.

French, *Choufleur.* German, *Blumenkohl.* Spanish, *Coliflor.*

CULTURE.—One ounce will produce three thousand plants. The cultural directions given for Cabbage will apply to this crop, but the soil should be more heavily manured. Keep them well hoed, and bring the earth gradually up to the stems. Water freely in dry weather, and especially when they begin to head. Never allow the plants to become crowded in the seed-bed; transplant them with great care, as any check will injure, if not entirely prevent, the formation of the head.

Extra-Early Dwarf Erfurt. For earliness and delicacy of flavor this has no equal; without exception the best variety grown . . . . per pkt., 50 cts. . $5 00

SNOWBALL CAULIFLOWER.

	Oz.	¼-lb.	Lb.
Early Dwarf Erfurt. Described in most catalogues as above, but much inferior to our extra-early strain, which we recommend . . . . per pkt., 15 cts. .	1 50	$5 00	$19 00
Early London. Large, and recommended for early use	40	1 00	3 50
Early Paris. Desirable as a second early	60	2 00	7 50
Large Algiers. Extra-fine, late variety, and a sure header	50	1 50	5 00
Lenormand. Short-stemmed, late sort, with very heavy heads	60	2 00	7 50
Snowball. Grown from Henderson's stock. One of the best early varieties in cultivation; fine, white heads of delicious flavor; sure header, and a great favorite	1 25	4 00	15 00
Veitch's Autumn Giant. Very large, firm, white heads; choice late sort	40	1 25	4 00

Our Collections of Plants and Bulbs are of great value; see second page of cover.

Celery.

French, *Celeri.* German, *Sellerie.* Spanish, *Apio.*

CULTURE.—One ounce will produce seven thousand plants. Sow in light, rich soil, in shallow drills, and cover the seed lightly with finely-sifted mold. Prick the seedlings out into beds of very rich soil, three inches apart. Water freely and shade from sun until established. When the plants are five to six inches high, transplant to rows three to four feet apart, according to the variety, allowing eight inches between the plants in the row. Cultivate freely and earth up to blanch the stems, pressing the soil firmly around the plant almost to the top. Remember that this crop well repays generous treatment.

	Oz.	¼-lb.	Lb.
Boston Market. An old favorite; tender, crisp and of mild flavor	$0 20	$0 50	$1 50
Giant Pascal. A recent introduction of great merit; solid, crisp, and of a rich, nutty flavor	40	1 25	4 00
Golden Heart. Dwarf; ordinary	20	50	1 50
Golden Self-Blanching. An early sort, of a rich golden color and exquisite flavor; easily blanched	25	75	2 50
Kalamazoo. A large, ribbed, good half-dwarf; favorite market sort	20	50	1 50
Pacific Pink. No better variety offered; solid, crisp, and of a delicious, nutty flavor	50	1 50	5 00
Perfection Heartwell. A regular heavy-weight variety of more than ordinary merit; deliciously crisp, and of exquisite flavor	30	75	2 50
White Plume. An excellent early variety; tender, crisp; of mild, pleasing flavor; not a good keeper	30	75	2 50

CELERIAC.

	Oz.	¼-lb.	Lb.
Large Smooth Prague. A variety of Celery with turnip shaped roots, white-fleshed, comparatively tender, with the flavor of Celery-stalks	25	75	2 50

Chervil.

French, *Cerfeuil.* German, *Garten-Kerbel.* Spanish, *Perifollo.*

CULTURE.—One ounce will sow fifty feet of drill. Sow in rows one foot apart, and cover very lightly. When the plants show themselves, thin out to eight inches apart in the drills. If cut down close the stems will soon sprout again.

	Oz.	¼-lb.	Lb.
Curled. Used in soups and salads; also for garnishing	$0 15	$0 40	$1 00
Tuberous-Rooted. A variety with edible roots	20	75	2 50

Chicory.

French, *Chicorée.* German, *Sichorie.* Spanish, *Endivia.*

CULTURE.—One ounce will sow one hundred feet of drill. Sow in rich soil in rows one foot apart, and thin to nine inches in the row. In the fall lift the roots, pack in boxes and blanch in dark cellar. The leaf-growth furnishes a delicious salad, or may be cooked in the same manner as Sea-kale.

	Oz.	¼-lb.	Lb.
Common (*Barbe de Capucine*). Much prized as a salad	$0 10	$0 30	$1 00
Large-Rooted. Roots of this variety are used as a substitute for coffee	10	30	1 00

CELERIAC.

If you use Celery, get a packet of Perfection Heartwell.

Corn.

SWEET or SUGAR.

French, *Mais*. German, *Welschkorn*. Spanish, *Maiz*.

CULTURE.—One pound will plant one hundred hills; eight pounds will plant one acre. Plant in hills three feet apart each way, covering about half an inch, and thin out to three plants to a hill. Field varieties should be planted four feet apart each way.

	Pkt.	Lb.	100 lbs.
Black Mexican. Late; very sweet, and of excellent flavor	$0 10	$0 13	$9 50
Early Crosby. One of the best early sorts; of dwarf habit good-sized ears	10	11	8 00
Early Minnesota. Small ears of excellent quality; very productive	10	11	8 00
Extra-Early Cory. Very early; good-sized ears; large kernels	10	12	9 00
Hickox Improved. A superb sort, with large, well-filled ears; very sweet	10	12	9 00
Late Mammoth. The largest variety grown; excellent for market	10	12	8 00
Perry's Hybrid. Very early; large size; succulent and tender	10	12	9 00
Stowell's Evergreen. A favorite late, sweet variety; remains tender a long time	10	12	8 00

FIELD CORN.

	Pkt.	Lb.	100 lbs.
Early Canada. Ears small, eight-rowed; very early	$0 10	$0 08	$7 00
Dakota Dent. The earliest variety grown; a superior selection	10	08	7 50
Leaning White. Very productive; deep grains and hardly any cob	10	08	7 50
Pride of the North. A very early yellow Dent	10	09	8 00
Yellow Flint. Produces large, handsome ears; very prolific	10	08	7 00
POP-CORN, Rice. Well-known variety; used for parching	10	07	6 00
POP-CORN, White Pearl. An improvement on the old white	10	06	5 00

Corn-Salad or Fetticus.

French, *Mache*. German, *Stechsalat*. Spanish, *Canonigos*.

CULTURE.—One ounce will sow sixty feet of drill. Mellow, rich soil, in a rather open situation, best suits this crop. The drills should be six inches apart and very shallow, not more than a quarter of an inch deep. Thin the plants to a distance of four inches in the row, and keep well cultivated.

	Oz.	¼-lb.	Lb.
Large-Seeded. The best variety for general use	$0 10	$0 25	$0 75

Cress or Pepper-Grass.

French, *Cresson*. German, *Kresse*. Spanish, *Mastuerzo*.

CULTURE.—One ounce will sow one hundred feet of drill. Sow thickly in shallow drills about six inches apart; repeat at short intervals, as it soon runs to seed. The seed of Water-cress should be scattered by the side of running water or near springs, and is soon in full bearing and lasts a long time.

	Oz.	¼-lb.	Lb.
Extra-Curled. Of beautiful appearance and fine flavor	$0 10	$0 15	$0 50
True Water-Cress. Mild and tender	50	1 50	5 00

TRUE WATER-CRESS.

Don't forget that Postage on Corn is 8 cents per pound.

Cucumbers.

French, *Concombre*. German, *Gurke*. Spanish, *Pepino*.

CULTURE.—One ounce will plant one hundred hills; two pounds will plant one acre. They succeed best in a warm, moist, rich, loamy soil. Plant in hills four feet apart each way. Leave four of the strongest plants to each hill, but do not thin out until plants are strong enough to resist the attacks of insects. The English forcing varieties can be grown in hot-beds where the temperature does not fall below sixty-five degrees at night. Many of this class grow from twenty to thirty inches in length.

	Oz.	¼-lb.	Lb.
Boston Pickling. Of uniform size; dark green, tender and productive	$0 10	$0 25	$0 75
Early Cluster. Excellent variety; very productive; grows in clusters	10	25	75
Early Russian. One of the earliest; fruit small and produced in pairs	10	25	75
Extra-Long Green. Handsome in shape and color; very desirable	10	30	1 00
Gherkin. Used only for pickles. Known also as West India Burr	20	60	2 00
Green Prolific. Resembles Boston Pickling, but much earlier	10	25	75
Improved White Spine. Very popular; flesh crisp and of good flavor	10	25	75
Nichol's Medium Green. Of beautiful color; very uniform in shape and size	10	30	1 00
Thorburn's Everbearing. Very early and enormously productive; the peculiar merit of this variety is that the vines continue to flower and produce fruit, whether the ripe Cucumbers are picked off or not, thus becoming almost a perpetual bearer	30	1 00	3 00

ENGLISH FRAME CUCUMBERS—These require to be grown in a frame or greenhouse, and, so provided for, produce wonderfully large and fine fruits. The varieties offered are the best known. Duke of Edinburgh, Telegraph, Tender and True, and Sion House Improved . . . . each, per pkt., 25 cts. .

Dandelion.

French, *Pissenlit*. German, *Pardeblum*. Spanish, *Amargon*.

CULTURE.—One ounce will sow two hundred feet of drill. Sow in drills half an inch deep and twelve inches apart, and thin out the plants to twelve inches. When about one year established the leaves may be cut, and form a most desirable spring salad. The roots, when dried and roasted, are often employed as a substitute for coffee.

	Oz.	¼-lb.	Lb.
Improved Large-Leaved. Twice the size of the common variety	$0 40	$1 50	$5 00

Egg-Plant.

French, *Aubergine*. German, *Eierpflanze*. Spanish, *Berengena*.

CULTURE.—One ounce will produce two thousand plants. A strong, uniform heat is required to germinate these seeds, and a thoroughly pulverized, well-enriched soil is necessary to perfect the fruit in. Transplant to three feet apart each way, and when about a foot high, support the plants by drawing earth up around them.

	Oz.	¼-lb.	Lb.
Black Pekin. Fruit round and solid, and jet-black	$0 50	$1 50	$5 00
Long Purple. Early; hardy and productive	30	1 00	3 50
New York Improved. The best; very large and of fine quality	50	1 50	5 00

EGG-PLANT.

Everbearing Cucumber is Worthy of a Trial.

Endive.

French, *Endive*. German, *Endivie*. Spanish, *Endibia*.

CULTURE.—One ounce will sow one hundred and fifty feet of drill. Sow in any ordinary dry soil, in drills one foot apart, covering lightly. When the plants are about two inches high, thin to about twelve inches in the row. When the plants have attained full size, gather up the leaves, tying together at the tips. This excludes the air from the inner leaves, which in the course of three or four weeks will become beautifully blanched.

	Oz.	¼-lb.	Lb.
Broad-leaved Batavian. A large summer variety; very productive, and one of the best	$0 20	$0 60	$2 00
Green Curled. Best for general use; very ornamental	20	50	1 50
White Curled. Similar to above; pale green foliage	20	60	2 00

ENDIVE.

Kale or Borecole.

French, *Chou vert Frise*. German, *Blatterkohl*. Spanish, *Cal*.

CULTURE.—One ounce will produce three thousand plants. With the exception of Sea Kale, the varieties under this heading are treated as directed for Cabbage, and transplanted from the seed-beds to permanent quarters, allowing two feet between each. Sow Sea Kale in drills one foot apart, and when ready transplant the roots, allowing two and a-half feet between each.

	Oz.	¼-lb.	Lb.
Dwarf Brown. Similar to the green, except in color	$0 10	$0 30	$1 00
Extra-Curled Scotch. Dwarf, compact grower; densely crisped green leaves	10	30	1 00
Improved Variegated. Highly ornamental foliage; useful for garnishing	25	75	2 50
Sea Kale. A splendid vegetable when blanched and eaten as Asparagus	25	75	2 50

KOHLRABI.

Kohlrabi. (Turnip-Rooted Cabbage.)

French, *Chou Rave*. German, *Kohlrabi*. Spanish, *Colinabo*.

CULTURE.—One ounce will produce twenty five hundred plants. Sow in rows eighteen inches apart, afterwards thinning to eight or ten inches. When young, Kohlrabi is a delicate and palatable vegetable, and is very popular in Germany and other countries of Europe, where it is more generally used than in the new world.

	Oz.	¼-lb.	Lb.
Early Purple Vienna. A favorite and successful table sort; largely grown	$0 30	$0 85	$3 00
Early White Vienna. The best variety; tender white flesh; very popular where known .	25	75	2 50
Large White or Green. Excellent variety for farm culture; finds a ready sale in the vegetable markets	15	50	1 50

KALE.

All packets in this Catalogue are 5 cents, except where noted.

Leek.

French, *Poireau.* German, *Lauch.* Spanish, *Puerro.*

CULTURE.—One ounce will sow one hundred feet of drill. Succeeds best in a light, rich soil. Sow in drills one inch deep and one foot apart ; when six or eight inches high transplant in rows ten inches apart and set deep, so as to blanch as much of the neck as possible.

	Oz.	¼-lb.	Lb.
American Large Flag. Of strong, vigorous growth ; the best of all	$0 20	$0 50	$1 75
Giant Carentan. A favorite European sort of mild flavor	20	50	1 75
Large Rouen. Grows to large size ; hardy and of excellent quality	20	50	1 75

LARGE ROUEN LEEK.

Lettuce.

French, *Laitue.* German, *Lattich.* Spanish, *Lechuga.*

CULTURE.—One ounce will sow two hundred feet of drill, and produce about two thousand plants. Sow thinly in rows one foot apart, and thin out to six or eight inches apart. To produce handsome heads of a crisp, tender quality, a very rich soil is necessary ; give plenty of water, and keep the soil thoroughly cultivated. If sown every two or three weeks, Lettuce may be had the entire season.

	Oz.	½-lb.	Lb.
California Cream Butter. Round solid heads of good size ; of a rich, buttery flavor	$0 20	$0 60	$2 00

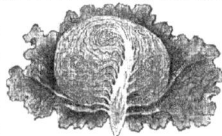

IMPROVED HANSON LETTUCE.

	Oz.	¼-lb.	Lb.
Curled Simpson, Black Seed. Superior variety ; twice the size of the white-seeded variety	$0 20	$0 50	$1 50
Curled Simpson, White Seed. Beautifully curled ; tender and crisp	15	40	1 25
Early Curled Silesia. Loose heads ; early and tender	15	40	1 25
Improved Hanson. Deliciously sweet ; very crisp and tender ; immense size	20	50	1 50
Mammoth Black-Seeded Butter. Very large heads ; close, crisp and delicious	30	1 00	3 00
Paris White Cos. (*Romaine.*) A French favorite ; of upright growth and good quality	15	40	1 25
Prize Head. Of superb flavor ; very tender and does not readily run to seed	$0 20	$0 60	$2 00
Salamander. Stands a greater amount of heat without running to seed than any other sort	20	50	1 50
Silver Ball. Firm, solid, attractive head ; rich, buttery flavor	20	50	1 50
Tennis Ball, Black Seed. Handsome heads ; crisp and tender	20	50	1 50
Tennis Ball or Boston, White Seed. Small-sized early sort	15	40	1 25
Trianon Self-Closing Cos. The best of all the Cos sorts ; stands heat well	30	1 00	3 00
White Summer Cabbage. Very popular ; of fairly good quality	15	40	1 25

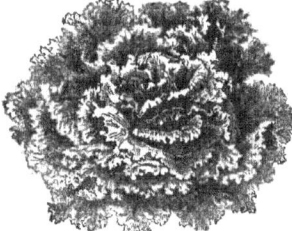

EARLY CURLED SILESIA LETTUCE.

Martynia.

German, *Gemsenhorn.*

CULTURE.—Sow in May in the open ground, three feet apart in each direction, where the plants are to remain ; or, the seed may be sown in a hotbed, and the seedlings afterward transplanted. Very productive and fine for pickles. Pick when small and tender, and preserve the same as cucumbers. Oz., 30 cts. ; ¼-lb., 75 cts. ; lb., $2.50.

Prize Head Lettuce is something that will please.

Melon, Musk.

French, *Melon Muscade.* German, *Cantalupen.* Spanish, *Muscotel.*

CULTURE.—One ounce will plant eighty hills; two pounds will plant an acre. A light, rich soil is essential for this crop. Plant in hills six feet apart each way, using ten to twelve seeds in the hill. After all danger of destruction by bugs is over, thin out to three plants to a hill, when about one foot long, pinch off the tips to make them branch. This strengthens the growth of the vines, and makes the fruit mature earlier.

EXTRA-EARLY HACKENSACK.

	Oz.	¼-lb.	Lb.
Bird's Cantaloup. Flesh thick, light green and of fine quality	$0 10	$0 25	$0 75
Delmonico. Oval shape; of large size, finely netted; beautiful orange-pink flesh	15	40	1 25
Emerald Gem. Distinct; very early; thick, salmon-colored flesh	10	25	75
Extra-Early Hackensack. Ten days earlier than the old variety; very desirable	10	25	75
Green Citron. Handsome round fruit; green flesh, melting and sweet; all the green-fleshed varieties are of superior flavor	10	25	75
Hybrid Bay View. Large, fine-flavored and a good shipper	10	25	75

	Oz.	¼-lb.	Lb.
Improved Orange Christiana. Very early; delicious, bright orange flesh	$0 15	$0 40	$1 25
Jenny Lind. Small, early; green-fleshed variety	10	25	75
Large Netted Cantaloup. Large, yellow-fleshed; old favorite	10	25	75
Mango Melon or Vegetable Orange. Size, shape and color of an orange; thick, meaty flesh; excellent for preserving	25	75	2 50
Miller's Cream. Delicious, rich salmon; flesh thick and solid	15	40	1 25
Nutmeg. Densely netted, deeply ribbed; green-fleshed variety	10	25	75
Skillman's Netted. Richly perfumed; deep green flesh of delicious flavor	10	25	75

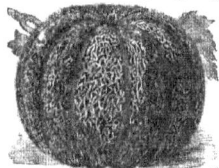

JENNY LIND.

	Oz.	¼-lb.	Lb.
Surprise. Oblong shape; rich orange flesh of fair quality	$0 10	$0 25	$0 75
Winter Pineapple. A recent introduction of delicious quality, to tickle the palate of lovers of fine fruit, and to prove a source of profit to enterprising and painstaking growers; of a rich, spicy flavor, peculiarly its own. The fruit should be picked in the fall, stored carefully in a quite cool place, and a few days before it is wanted for use, it should be placed in a warm room, where it will ripen for the table and prove an addition to the menu	25	75	2 50

EMERALD GEM.

Winter Pineapple is a Wonderful New Musk-Melon.

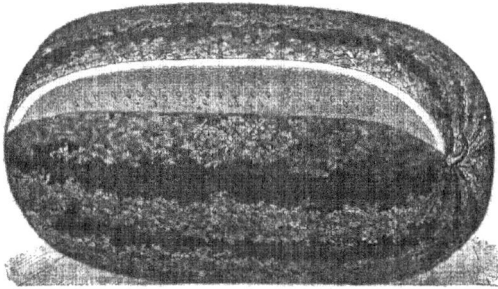

MAMMOTH IRONCLAD.

Melon, Water.

French, *Melon d'Eau.* German, *Wassermelone.* Spanish, *Zandia.*

CULTURE.—One ounce will plant thirty hills; four pounds will plant an acre. Treat as recommended for Musk-melon, except that the hills should not be less than eight feet apart.

	Oz.	¼-lb.	Lb.
Black Spanish. Solid, very thin rind; sweet, scarlet flesh	$0 10	$0 25	$0 75
Citron (for preserving). Red-seeded; small, round, handsome fruit	10	25	75
Cuban Queen. A magnificent variety, with bright red, luscious flesh	10	25	75
Green and Gold. Grows to good size; early, productive, and of good flavor	15	30	1 00
Jordan's Gray Monarch. Largest melon grown; sweet, crimson flesh; late	10	25	75
Kentucky Wonder. Beautiful scarlet; solid flesh; crisp, rich and sugary	15	30	1 00
Kolb's Gem. Light green, nearly round; rich, bright red, sweet flesh	10	25	75
Lodi or San Joaquin. Of uniform, medium size, pink flesh, sweet and delicious . . .	10	25	75

	Oz.	¼-lb.	Lb.
Mammoth Iron-clad. Large; flesh bright red, crisp and delicious	$0 10	$0 25	$0 75
Mountain Sweet. An old favorite; flesh solid, crisp and sweet . .	10	25	75
Phinney's Early. A medium-sized extra early sort; red flesh of excellent quality .	10	25	75
Pride of Georgia. Of good size; deep red, crisp, sweet flesh . .	10	25	75
Ruby Gold. A recent introduction; juicy and of superb flavor	15	30	1 00
Southern Rattle-snake or **Gipsy.** Large, oblong, striped and mottled; good shipper .	10	25	75

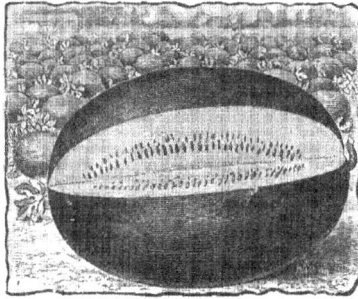

GREEN AND GOLD.

Mushroom Spawn.

French, *Blanc de Champignon.* German, *Champignonbrut.* Spanish, *Seta.*

CULTURE.—Ten pounds will spawn ten feet square. Mushrooms of excellent quality can be grown with ease almost the year round, the only requirement being unfermented manure, a small quantity of good soil, and reliable spawn. Full instructions on the preparation and management of the beds, will be found in "Mushroom Culture," by W. Robinson, which will be sent free by mail for fifty cents. Our spawn can be thoroughly depended on and being specially manufactured for us, is fresh and reliable at all times.

MUSHROOM SPAWN.

	Per lb.	100 lbs.
English Spawn. In bricks weighing ¾-lb. each	$0 20	$18 00
French Spawn. In 3-lb boxes . . . . . per box, $2 ; in bulk .	40	

Mustard.

French, *Moutarde.* German, *Senf.* Spanish, *Mostaza.*

CULTURE.—One ounce will sow a drill fifty feet long. Sow thickly in rows six inches apart, and when about two inches high it can be cut and used with Cress, forming a pleasing pungent salad.

	Oz.	¼-lb.	Lb.
Black or Brown. More pungent than the Yellow	$0 05	$0 10	$0 25
Chinese. Leaves twice the size of the ordinary ; sweet and pungent	10	25	75
White or Yellow. Of very rapid growth and agreeable flavor	05	10	25

CHINESE MUSTARD

Nasturtium.

French, *Capucine.* German, *Nasturtium.* Spanish, *Marancula.*

CULTURE.—One ounce will sow fifty feet of drill. Sow in drills one inch deep, the tall varieties by the side of a fence, trellis work or other support to climb upon. The seed pods, which resemble capers, are gathered while green and tender and used for pickling, and the leaves are used in salads.

	Oz.	¼-lb.	Lb.
Dwarf Mixed. All colors	$0 20	$0 50	$1 75
" **Scarlet**	25	60	2 00
" **Yellow**	25	60	2 00
Tall Mixed. All colors	10	30	1 00
" **Crimson**	20	50	1 50
" **Yellow**	10	30	1 00

OKRA.

Okra or Gombo.

French, *Gombaud.* German, *Safran.* Spanish, *Quimbombo.*

CULTURE.—One ounce will plant one hundred hills. Of easy cultivation in any good soil ; plant about two inches deep, in drills three feet apart, and when well established thin to three plants in the hill; keep the soil well worked, and occasionally draw a little up around the stalks to support them. The pods should be gathered while young and tender.

	Oz.	¼-lb.	Lb.
Dwarf Density. Best for general crop; tender long pods	$0 15	$0 35	$1 25
White Velvet. Handsome and productive ; long smooth white pods	10	25	75

If you want a Lawn, give a glance at second page of this Catalogue.

Spanish King.

Onions.

French, *Oignon.* German, *Zwiebel.* Spanish, *Cebolla.*

CULTURE.—One ounce will sow one hundred feet of drill; six pounds will plant one acre. A deep soil, thoroughly worked and as rich as possible, is best for this crop. Sow thinly in shallow drills about twelve inches apart; when the plants are about three inches high, thin to the distance of three or four inches, according to the variety.

	Oz.	¼-lb.	Lb.
Extra-Early Red Flat. Of fair size; very early and productive	$0 30	$0 90	$3 00
Extra-Early Red Globe. Similar to the above, except in shape	25	75	2 50
Giant Red Rocca. A magnificent variety of mild flavor	25	75	2 50
Giant White Tripoli. Of silvery white color and very pleasant flavor	25	75	2 50
Queen. Extra-early, small-sized variety; valuable for pickling	30	1 00	3 00
Red Globe. Deep red; fine-grained, firm flesh; keeps well	25	75	2 50
Silver King. Silvery white; one of the largest varieties grown	35	1 00	3 00
Spanish King. Of enormous size, the average weight being three pounds; reddish brown skin; flesh pure white, fine-grained and remarkably mild	40	1 25	4 00
Wethersfield Large Red. A favorite variety; good keeper	30	90	3 00
White Globe. Fine, white flesh of mild flavor	35	1 00	3 50
White Portugal or Silver Skin. A well-known large white variety	40	1 25	4 00
Yellow Danvers. Very productive; one of the best keepers	25	75	2 50
Yellow Globe. A leading variety; fine-grained and of mild flavor	30	90	3 00

Our "SELECTED SEEDS" are all new, and they are of good germinating power.

Onion Sets, Etc.

CULTURE.—Plant in drills twelve inches apart and four inches between the sets. Prices are subject to market fluctuations as the season advances.

Red Onion Sets	Market price
White " "	" "
Yellow " "	" "
Top Onions	" "
Garlic	" "
Potato-Onions	" "
Shallots	" "

Onion Sets.

Parsley.

French, *Persil.* German, *Petersilie.* Spanish, *Perejil.*

CULTURE.—One ounce will sow one hundred feet of drill. Sow thinly in drills one foot apart, and thin out the plants to three or four inches between each. The seed germinates slowly, sometimes three or four weeks passing before the plants show.

	Oz.	¼-lb.	Lb.
Champion Moss-Curled. Very select strain; compact and beautifully curled	$0 10	$0 30	$1 90
Fern-Leaved. A distinct and attractive dwarf variety; highly ornamental	15	40	1 00
Hamburg or **Rooted.** The fleshy roots of this variety are largely used for flavoring soups	15	40	1 00

Parsnip.

French, *Panais.* German, *Pastinake.* Spanish, *Chirivia.*

CULTURE.—One ounce will sow two hundred feet of drill; five pounds will plant an acre. This crop requires a very rich soil. Sow in drills eighteen inches apart, and thin to eight inches in the row. Besides being desirable as a table vegetable, they are valuable for feeding stock.

	Oz.	¼-lb.	Lb.
Improved Guernsey. Fine-grained; flesh of excellent quality	$0 10	$0 20	$0 60
Long Smooth or Hollow Crown. Of excellent flavor; tender and sweet	10	20	60
Student. Handsome shape and splendid flavor	10	20	60

Pepper.

French, *Piment.* German, *Pfeffer.* Spanish, *Pimiento.*

CULTURE.—One ounce will produce fifteen hundred plants. Good, rich, mellow ground is best for Peppers. Transplant into rows two feet between the plants each way. Keep the soil open and free with the cultivator.

	Oz.	¼-lb.	Lb.
Golden Dawn. Handsome, golden yellow; mild and sweet	$0 30	$0 90	$3 00
Large Bell or Bull-Nose. Early and of pleasing flavor	30	90	3 00
Large Squash. Very productive; fleshy and mild	25	75	2 50
Long Red Cayenne. Bright red pods; very pungent; prolific	30	90	3 00
Red Cherry. Small, round, bright scarlet pods; very hot	30	90	3 00
Red Chili. Bright red, cone-shaped pods; very pungent	30	90	3 00
Ruby King. Enormously productive and of immense size; of mild flavor .	30	90	3 00
Sweet Mountain. Large, early variety of mild flavor	25	75	2 50

RUBY KING PEPPER.

Public Institutions requiring large quantities supplied on special terms.

AMERICAN WONDER PEA.

Peas.

French, *Pois.* German, *Erbzen.* Spanish, *Chicaros o Guizantes.*

CULTURE.—One pound will sow sixty feet of row; one hundred pounds is required for an acre in drills. Light, moderately rich soil is best for this crop. They are generally sown in double rows six or eight inches apart, allowing four to six feet between the rows, according to the variety. Keep clean, and earth up twice during their growth. *Wrinkled varieties are marked thus* *.

	Height in ft.	Pkt.	Lb.	100 lbs.
Alaska. Extra-early; of good flavor and color	2½	$0 10	$0 12	$8 50
***American Wonder.** Extra-early; very productive and of superior flavor; a profitable variety for the grower 1		10	13	10 00
Black-Eyed Marrowfat. Extensively grown as a field pea 3		10	8	7 00
Blue Imperial. Prolific and of fine flavor 2½		10	9	8 00
Blue Peter. An early dwarf, with well-filled, large pods . . . . ⅔		10	13	10 00
***Champion of England.** The most popular pen in cultivation; of superior quality and great productiveness 5		10	8	6 00
Daniel O'Rourke Improved. A valuable extra-early; productive and good; a universal favorite 2½		10	12	9 00
***Everbearing.** Handsome pods, well filled with large peas of superior flavor; a good market variety 2½		10	13	10 00
First and Best. A market favorite; early and productive 2½		10	11	8 00
***Little Gem.** Productive, and of delicious flavor 1		10	12	9 00
***McLean's Advancer.** A standard early sort of excellent quality 2½		10	12	9 00
Niles or Small White. A well-known variety, largely used for field culture . . . . market prices per lb. and 100 lbs. . 3		10		
Philadelphia Extra-Early. Very productive and of good flavor 3		10	11	8 00
***Premium Gem.** Larger pods and more productive than Little Gem 1		10	13	9 00
***Stratagem.** An excellent, late marrow; very large pods; of exquisite flavor; destined to great popularity 1½		10	13	9 00
Sugar, Dwarf. Young pods used like string beans; tender and sweet 2½		10	40	
Sugar, Tall. Similar to the preceding except in height 5		10	40	
***Telephone.** Immense pods; very productive and of superior flavor 4		10	12	9 00
Tom Thumb. A well-known dwarf variety of fair quality 1		10	13	10 00
White Marrowfat. A favorite sort; produces large, well-filled pods 4		10	8	7 00
***Yorkshire Hero.** A very prolific, deliciously-flavored, late Pea 2½		10	10	7 00

Don't forget that Postage on Peas is 8 cents per pound.

Pumpkin.

French, *Potiron* German, *Kürbis.* Spanish, *Calabaza.*

CULTURE.—One ounce will plant forty hills; five pounds will plant an acre. Plant in hills eight or ten feet apart each way, allowing four seeds to a hill. In other respects they are cultivated as melons and cucumbers.

	Oz.	¼-lb.	Lb.
Connecticut Field or Large Yellow. The best for field culture and for feeding stock	$0 10	$0 20	$0 50
Early Sugar. Fine-grained; sweet and prolific	10	25	75
Large Cheese. Flesh fine-grained, sweet and well flavored, a favorite for making pies	10	25	75
Mammoth Potiron. Salmon-colored skin; flesh fine-grained and of excellent quality; grows to enormous size	20	60	2 00

LARGE CHEESE PUMPKIN.

Radish.

French, *Radis.* German, *Rettig.* Spanish, *Rabanitos*

CULTURE —One ounce will sow one hundred feet of drill; two pounds will be required for one acre. Radishes do best in a light, rich soil Sow in drills about ten inches apart, covering about half an inch, and thin the plants to two inches apart. A rapid growth is essential to produce showy, crisp radishes of a mild flavor. Sow every ten days for a succession of crops.

	Oz.	¼-lb.	Lb.
Black Spanish, Long. Of large size; firm, solid, crisp flesh; keeps well	$0 10	$0 25	$0 75
Black Spanish, Round. Globe-shaped; of good quality and flavor	10	25	75
Chartier Improved. A long, white-tipped sort; handsome and of good quality	10	20	60
Chinese Rose. In shape, half-long; bright pink color; solid flesh and of good flavor	10	25	75
Early White Turnip. Very early, crisp and good	10	25	75
Extra-Early Roman Carmine. The best of all; early, crisp and delicious	10	25	75
French Breakfast. Attractive in appearance and of rapid growth	10	20	60
Long Scarlet Short-Top. A standard sort; very long; color bright scarlet	10	20	60

	Oz	¼-lb.	Lb.
Long White Vienna or Lady's Finger. The sweetest long white Radish grown; a popular variety	$0 10	$0 25	$0 75
Mammoth White China. Flesh pure white; of good flavor and keeps well	10	30	1 00
Olive-Shaped Scarlet. Of bright color; mild and fine; a very good sort	10	25	75
Scarlet Turnip. Largely grown; very early, sweet and crisp, a fine market variety	10	20	60
Scarlet Turnip, White-Tipped. Differs from the preceding in color only	10	20	60
White Strasburgh. A rapid-growing, large sort; flesh sweet, and never pithy	10	25	75
Wood's Early Frame. Rich crimson color; matures quickly; very crisp and sweet, and one of the most popular sorts	10	20	60
Yellow Summer Turnip. Large, yellow-skinned variety of good flavor	10	25	75

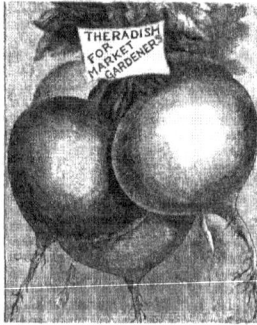

THE RADISH FOR MARKET GARDENERS

TYPE OF THE TURNIP RADISHES.

All Seeds are 5 cents per packet, except where noted.

Rhubarb.

French, *Rhubarbe.* German, *Rhabarber.* Spanish, *Ruibarbo.*

CULTURE.—One ounce will sow one hundred and twenty-five feet of drill. The seed-bed should be of light, rich soil. Sow very thinly in rows one foot apart, and cover the seed about one inch. When the plants are two inches high, thin to the distance of six inches in the drill. In about six months they will be strong enough to set out in their permanent location, the distance allowed being about three feet each way.

	Oz.	¼-lb.	Lb.
Linnæus	$0 20	$0 50	$1 75
Mammoth Monarch	25	75	2 50
Victoria	20	50	1 75

Roots of either variety, $1.50 per dozen, by express, at purchaser's expense.

Salsify or Vegetable Oyster.

French, *Salsifis.* German, *Haferwurzel.* Spanish, *Ostra Vegetal.*

CULTURE.—One ounce will sow a drill sixty feet; five pounds will sow one acre. The soil should be rich and well worked to a depth of eighteen inches at least. Sow in drills fifteen inches apart, covering the seeds with fine soil an inch and a-half in depth. When the plants are strong enough, thin them out to about nine inches apart.

LINNÆUS RHUBARB.

	Oz.	¼-lb.	Lb.
Large White French. Small-growing, but of good flavor	$0 10	$0 40	$1 25
Mammoth Sandwich Island. Distinct, and a great improvement on the old variety; roots well-formed and very large	15	50	1 50
Scorzonera or Long Black. A Spanish variety, used in soups	20	50	2 00

Sorrel.

French, *Oseille.* German, *Sauerampfer.* Spanish, *Acedera.*

CULTURE.—One ounce will sow one hundred and fifty feet of drill. Sow in rows fifteen inches apart and one-half inch deep. Thin the seedlings out to ten inches apart in the row.

	Oz.	¼-lb.	Lb.
French Broad-Leaved. Of pleasing acidity; much valued	$0 15	$0 40	$1 25

Spinach.

French, *Épinard.* German, *Spinat.* Spanish, *Espinaca.*

CULTURE.—One ounce will sow one hundred feet of drill; ten pounds will sow one acre. An exceedingly rich, well-worked soil is necessary. Sow thinly in drills ten inches apart and half an inch deep. When the young plants are established, thin out to the distance of three or four inches in the row, and in a future thinning every alternate plant may be removed, as Spinach does not do well when crowded.

SALSIFY.

	Oz.	¼-lb.	Lb.
Long-Standing. Round, thick leaves, of a dark green color	$0 10	$0 15	$0 40
Prickly. A very hardy variety; strongly recommended	10	15	40
Perpetual or Spinach Beet. Produces a great abundance of green leaves, and as soon as one gathering has been made, a fresh crop appears, thus insuring a constant supply of this valuable vegetable	$0 10	$0 25	$0 75
Round Thick-Leaved. Of good quality; a favorite market sort	10	15	40
Savoy-Leaved or Bloomsdale. Large, thick, succulent, curled leaves	10	15	40
Viroflay. A large-leaved variety; grown largely in many localities	10	15	40

SAVOY-LEAVED SPINACH.

"QUALITY" is our watchword, and our Prices are Reasonable.

PERFECT GEM.

ESSEX HYBRID.

Squash.

French, *Courge.* German, *Küchen Kurbis.* Spanish, *Calabaza.*

CULTURE —One ounce will plant fifty hills ; four to six pounds, according to variety, is required for one acre. Plant in well-manured hills, the bush varieties three or four feet apart, and the running sorts from six to eight feet. Eight or ten seeds should be allowed to a hill, thinning out after danger of bugs is over, and leaving three or four of the strongest plants to a hill.

PIKE'S PEAK.

	Oz.	¼-lb.	Lb.
Boston Marrow. Bright orange skin ; flesh of excellent quality . .	$0 10	$0 25	$0 75
Californian Field Marrow. Largely grown for stock feeding ; an enormous quantity can be produced per acre, and the squashes form a most excellent and nutritious food for cattle	5	15	40
Early White Scallop Bush. The best early, and very productive ; of an attractive shape and color	10	25	75
Essex Hybrid. Very prolific ; fine-grained, sweet, dry flesh	10	25	75

	Oz.	¼-lb.	Lb.
Hubbard. A popular late sort of superior quality	$0 10	$0 25	$0 75
Mammoth Chili. Of immense size ; rich, thick flesh of good quality	25	75	2 50
Marblehead. Resembles Hubbard, but has gray-green skin	10	25	75
Perfect Gem. A productive, round, white variety of fine quality	10	25	75
Pike's Peak. Flesh fine-grained ; rich and delicate in flavor ; has also been known as "Sibley"	10	25	75
Pineapple. A late variety of peculiar shape, as may be seen by the illustration ; white skin and flesh	10	25	75
Summer Crookneck. A good summer sort ; golden skin, warted ; of especially fine and delicate flavor	10	25	75
Vegetable Marrow. A delicious English variety, with white, soft flesh of a rich flavor ; quite distinct from all other sorts, and well worth attention	15	40	1 25

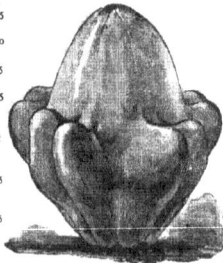

PINEAPPLE SQUASH.

Our Menlo Park Lawn Grass (see page 2) is unsurpassed.

Tomato.

French, *Tomato*. German, *Liebesapfel.* Spanish, *Tomates.*

CULTURE.—One ounce will produce fifteen hundred plants ; four ounces will produce enough for one acre. They do best on a light, warm, not over-rich soil, and success depends to a very great extent in securing a rapid, vigorous, unchecked growth the early part of the season. Transplant as soon as the plants are fit to handle into shallow boxes, setting them four or five inches apart. When strong and stocky, set out in hills four feet apart. By training the vines on trellises or other supports they will be more productive, and the fruit will be of much better quality.

	Oz.	¼-lb.	Lb.
Acme. Early ; of medium size ; pink skin ; solid flesh ; good bearer	$0 25	$0 75	$2 50
Beauty (Livingston's). Large, smooth, glossy, purple-crimson color ; very solid	25	75	2 50
Dwarf Champion. A valuable recent introduction; of dwarf, stiff habit, requires very little support ; color same as Acme ; very early, smooth, and of medium size	30	85	3 00
Favorite (Livingston's). Handsome shape ; of good size ; solid, seedless flesh	25	75	2 50
Ignotum. Of uniform size and shape ; heavy and solid ; earliest of the large sorts	30	85	3 00
Long-Keeper (Thorburn's). A new, very early and productive variety ; free from rot, and remarkable for its long-keeping qualities . . . . . per pkt., 15 cts.	50		
Mikado. A very large early sort ; purplish red color ; solid and good	25	75	2 50
New Jersey. Large, solid, smooth and bright red ; one of the very best	25	75	2 50

Peach. Very distinct ; fruit resembles a peach in shape, size, bloom and color, which is a deep orange-rose ; flesh solid, and unsurpassed in flavor ; this is a most interesting and unique variety, which will probably lead to a new race of Tomatoes 30 85 3 00

Perfection (Livingston's). A favorite everywhere ; bright scarlet ; solid and rich 25 75 2 50

	Oz.	¼-lb.	Lb.
Red Cherry. Fruit about an inch in diameter ; very showy when used in pickles	$0 35	$1 00	$3 50
Strawberry or **Ground-Cherry.** Enormously productive ; small, yellow fruits of very sweet flavor, which make a most enjoyable preserve	35	1 00	3 50
Trophy. Large and solid ; unsurpassed in flavor and productiveness ; has been a standard variety for many years	25	75	2 50
Yellow Plum. Handsome variety ; skin and flesh deep yellow	30	85	3 00

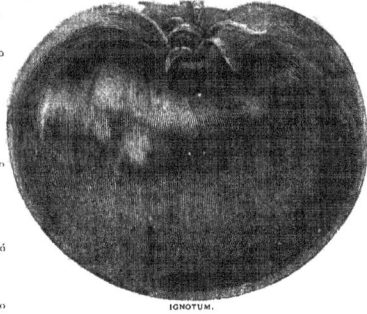

ACME.

IGNOTUM.

We sell Tomato, Cabbage and Celery Plants in season.

Turnip.

French, *Navet.* German, *Rüben.* Spanish, *Nabo.*

CULTURE.—One ounce will sow one hundred and fifty feet of drill; two pounds will sow one acre. This crop does best in highly enriched, light, sandy soil. Sow in drills from twelve to fifteen inches, and thin early to eight or nine inches apart. A good crop when cultivated with judgment.

WHITE EGG.

	Oz.	¼-lb.	Lb.
Extra-Early Purple-Top Milan. Earliest in cultivation; white flesh of excellent flavor	$0 10	$0 25	$0 75
Golden Ball or Orange Jelly. Very handsome; rich, pale yellow flesh	10	20	60
Purple-Top Munich. A very early sort; snow-white flesh, of excellent flavor	10	20	60
Red-Top Globe. A standard variety; very heavy cropper	10	20	60
Sweet German. A long variety; flesh pure white, solid, sweet and mild-flavored	10	25	75
White Egg. Skin and flesh of snowy whiteness; sweet, firm and fine-grained	10	20	60
White Flat Dutch. Very early; white flesh; solid and mild	10	20	60
White French or Rock. Grows long; sweet and mild-flavored	10	25	75

	Oz.	¼-lb.	Lb.
White Norfolk. Grows to a large size; used mostly for feeding stock	$0 10	$0 15	$0 50
White Strap-Leaf. A good, early, white variety; fine flavor	10	20	60
Yellow Aberdeen. Good keeper; usually grown for stock feeding	10	20	60
Yellow Stone. The best yellow-fleshed variety for table use; delicious quality	10	25	75

Ruta-Baga.

IMPROVED RUTA BAGA

	Oz.	¼-lb.	Lb.
Improved American. Solid flesh of superior quality; good for table or stock	$0 10	$0 25	$0 75
Champion Purple-Top. Highly recommended; produces extraordinary crops in good soil	10	20	60
Laing's Improved. Handsome variety of excellent quality	10	20	60
Prize-Winner. Of large size and very symmetrical; keeps sound and good for a long time	10	20	60
Shamrock. Productive and nutritious; excellent for stock feeding	10	20	60
Skirving's Purple-Top. A first-rate variety, and keeps well	10	20	60

If you receive two Catalogues, give your neighbor one.

SWEET BASIL.   SAGE.   SWEET MARJORAM. SUMMER SAVORY,   THYME.

Herbs and Medicinal Plants.

CULTURE.—This class of plants does best in mellow, and not too rich soil. The best general directions for sowing are, to cover the seeds about twice their own thickness; when up, thin the plants out, so that they may have sufficient light and air, and not be so crowded as to get into a drawn and unhealthy condition. When harvesting, cut on a dry day, when not quite in full blossom. Dry quickly in the shade, and pack in close boxes, keeping them entirely excluded from the air. Varieties marked * are perennials, and when once established may be preserved in the garden for years with but little care. A bed of these useful plants is highly desirable at any farm or country place.

	Oz.	¼-lb.	Lb.
Anise (*Pimpinella Anisum*). The seeds are used for garnishing and flavoring, and in confectionery; very aromatic	$0 15	$0 35	$1 00
*Balm (*Melissa officinalis*). Very fragrant; used as a tea in fevers	50	1 25	4 00
Basil, Sweet (*Ocymum basilicum*). The leaves are used for flavoring soups, stews, etc.	25	75	2 50
Belladonna (*Atropa Belladonna*). Used in medicine	50	1 50	5 00
Bene (*Sesamum orientale*). Leaves are used in medicine for dysentery and diarrhœa	15	50	1 50
Borage (*Borago officinalis*). Flowers furnish excellent bee pasture	15	35	1 00
*Caraway (*Carum Carui*). Seeds extensively used in flavoring bread, pastry, etc.; they have a strong individual flavor	10	20	50
Catnip (*Nepeta cataria*). Well-known for its medicinal qualities	50	1 25	4 00
Coriander (*Coriandrum sativum*). Seeds are very aromatic, and are extensively used in confectionery, flavoring, etc.	10	20	50
Dill (*Anethum graveolens*). Aromatic, pungent and medicinal	15	30	1 00
*Fennel, Sweet (*Anethum Fœniculum*). Leaves largely used in fish sauce	10	20	75
Hyssop (*Hyssopus officinale*). Used medicinally for colds and lung troubles	20	60	2 00
*Horehound (*Marrubium vulgare*). A popular cure for coughs, colds, etc.; also used as flavoring for confectionery	30	75	3 00
*Lavender (*Lavandula vera*). Of delicious fragrance; for oil and distilled water; the leaves and stems are also prized for scenting clothing and linen	20	50	1 50
Marigold, Pot (*Calendula officinalis*) Used in soups	15	50	1 50
Marjoram, Sweet (*Origanum Majorana*). Highly esteemed for flavoring; very fragrant and aromatic	25	75	2 50
*Pennyroyal (*Mentha pulegium*). Very ornamental, and of high medicinal qualities; the oil extracted is of great commercial value	75	1 50	6 00
*Rosemary (*Rosmarinus officinalis*). Yields aromatic oil and water	40	1 00	3 50
*Rue (*Ruta graveolens*). Medicinal use, and used by poultry raisers for croup	20	50	1 50
Saffron (*Carthamus tinctorius*). Used in medicine, and for dyeing	10	20	75
*Sage (*Salvia officinalis*). Used extensively for seasoning and dressing	20	50	1 50
Summer Savory (*Satureja Hortensis*). Used extensively for flavoring soups, etc.	20	50	1 50
*Tansy (*Tanacetum vulgare*). Generally used for bitters	30	75	3 00
*Thyme (*Thymus vulgaris*). Tea of this is a well-known and popular remedy for nervous headaches	40	1 00	3 75
*Wormwood (*Artemisia Absinthium*). Has high medicinal qualities	30	75	3 00

"QUALITY" is our watchword, and prices are reasonable.

SELECTED GRASS AND CLOVER SEEDS

For Menlo Park Lawn Grass and Other Mixtures, see page 2.

GRASS SEED.

The grass and clover seeds offered by us are all of the best grades, and have been specially recleaned to meet the demands of our critical trade. Prices for large quantities will be quoted on application. This is more satisfactory than quoting here, as prices are subject to frequent changes with market fluctuations.

Per lb.

Bermuda Grass (*Cynodon dactylon*). No more valuable grass for summer pasture can be grown; it is easily cultivated, stands the drought well, is very nutritious, gives splendid green pasture for eight months of the year, and an average yield of three to four tons per acre. Sow at the rate of ten pounds per acre $1 25

Crested Dog's-tail (*Cynosurus cristatus*). An excellent grass for hard, dry soils; of exceeding value also for pastures and lawns. When it is used alone, twenty-five pounds of this seed is required per acre 60

Fescue, Slender (*Festuca tenuifolia*). Valuable as a mixture with grasses for lawns, and does well on dry, sterile soils 60

Fescue, Meadow (*Festuca pratensis*). An excellent pasture grass, its long, tender leaves being much relished by cattle; succeeds best as a mixture with other grasses, but if sown alone, forty pounds to the acre is required 25

Fescue, Hard (*Festuca duriuscula*). Will thrive in a great variety of soils, and resist the effect of drought in a remarkable degree; from the fineness of its foliage it is well adapted for lawns or sheep pasture. Sow thirty pounds per acre 40

Fescue, Sheep (*Festuca ovina*). In bulk of produce this variety falls short of the other Fescues, but should enter into the composition of all mixtures for sheep pastures, as they are very fond of this grass. If sown alone, thirty-five pounds is required for an acre 35

Hungarian Grass (*Panicum Germanicum*). A valuable annual soiling and forage plant, that grows well on almost any soil. Sow at the rate of seventy pounds per acre 10

JOHNSON GRASS.

Johnson Grass (*Sorghum Halepense*). One of the most valuable rapid-growing fodder plants known; on rich soil it can be cut three or four times a season; the hay is rich, juicy and tender, and relished by stock. Sow at the rate of thirty-five pounds per acre 20

Kentucky Blue Grass, Fancy Clean (*Poa pratensis*). This is the best pasture grass for our climate and soil, and produces the most nourishing food for cattle; although it yields herbage early, it requires several years to become well established as a pasture grass. Thirty pounds of seed required for one acre 25

Per lb.

Mesquite or Velvet Grass (*Holcus lanatus*). Has the merit of easy culture, and accommodates itself to all descriptions of soils, from the richest to the poorest. Forty pounds is required for one acre $0 10

Millet, Common. Grows from three to four feet high, with broad blades and strong stalks, affording excellent pasturage. For pasturage sow thirty pounds per acre, but if intended for seed, half that quantity will be sufficient for that area of soil . . . .

Millet, German. More prolific than the preceding variety; yields from two to three thousand pounds of seed per acre, which is excellent feed for stock or poultry 10

Millet, Pearl (*Penicellaria spicata*). Distinct from the two preceding varieties, and one of the most luxuriant-growing fodder plants we know of; when cultivated for fodder, the seed should be dropped in drills three feet apart, and given plenty of room on account of its tillering habit; it is in best condition for cutting when the stalks are five or six feet high. Five pounds will sow an acre . . . .

10 KENTUCKY BLUE GRASS.

We will send ten varieties California Tree Seeds for $1.

GRASS SEED, Continued.

Per lb.

Oat Grass, Tall Meadow (*Avena elatior*). Highly recommended for mixtures for permanent pastures in dry, gravelly soils; produces an abundant supply of foliage, and is valuable on account of its early and luxuriant growth. Fifty pounds will sow an acre $0 35

Orchard Grass (*Dactylis glomerata*). The most valuable and widely known of all pasture grasses, coming earlier in the spring and remaining longer than any other; it is well adapted for sowing under trees, and valuable either for grazing or for hay. Forty pounds is required for one acre 20

Reana luxurians (*Teosinte*). In appearance this gigantic gramina of Central America somewhat resembles Indian corn, but the leaves are much larger and broader, and the stalks contain sweeter sap; eighty-five stalks have been grown from one seed. Forty-five pounds will sow one acre 1 75

Red-Top (*Agrostis vulgaris*). A valuable permanent grass for meadows or lawns, growing in almost any soil, moist or dry, and standing heat well. Forty-five pounds to the acre 12

Red-Top, Absolutely Clean. Cannot be surpassed in quality 20

Rye Grass, Perennial (*Lolium perenne*). Enters largely into the composition of many of the richest pastures, and is one of the most nutritious of the permanent grasses. Forty pounds for one acre 15

Rye Grass, Italian (*Lolium Italicum*). Similar to the preceding, but of more rapid growth, which is its chief merit. Fifty pounds will sow one acre 12

Sweet Vernal (*Anthoxanthum odoratum*). We offer only the true perennial variety of this valuable grass; useful for mixing with other grasses for lawns and meadows, on account of the early growth and the fragrance which the leaves emit when cut for hay. When sown alone, twenty pounds per acre is required 75

OAT GRASS.

Timothy (*Phleum pratense*). Well-known and extensively grown; very productive, and thrives on almost any soil, and on a moist clay will produce a larger crop than any other grass. From twenty-five to forty pounds is used per acre 10

Per lb.

Wood Meadow Grass (*Poa nemoralis*). A very productive and nutritious grass; thrives well in moist, shady situations or under trees. Thirty pounds is required for one acre $0 50

CLOVER SEED.

Per lb.

Alfalfa or Lucerne (*Medicago sativa*). Succeeds well in almost any location, and lasts for a number of years; it grows two or three feet high, and the roots extend deeply into the soil, which enables it to resist the severest drought; it produces heavy crops of nutritious foliage, which may be cut three or four times a year, the best time being just when commencing to bloom. Sow ten pounds to the acre $0 20

Alsike (*Trifolium hybridum*). Thrives well on rich, moist soils, and yields an enormous bulk of forage much preferred by cattle; may be cut several times a season, and as an addition to mixtures for permanent pastures has no superior. Sow ten pounds to the acre 30

RED-TOP GRASS.

There may be something in our Plant Department that you are looking for.

CLOVER SEED, Continued.

Per lb.

Japan Clover (*Lespedeza striata*). A branching perennial, growing about twelve inches high, and in warm latitudes will do well in any soil, even during extreme drought; more nutritious than Red Clover, and makes excellent hay $0 40

Mammoth Pea Vine. Largely used for plowing under for manure, and for reclaiming exhausted lands; will grow where the common clovers fail, but the stalks are so coarse that stock eat only the leaves. Eight pounds per acre is generally used . . . . Market price; write for quotations .

Medium Red (*Trifolium pratense*). A well-known standard; excellent for pasturage or hay, and should be in all grass mixtures. If sown alone, ten pounds per acre is required . . . . Market price; write for quotations .

White Dutch (*Trifolium repens*). A spreading perennial; valuable for pastures and lawns; it accommodates itself to a variety of soils, but prefers moist ground; is excellent food for bees. Six pounds will sow one acre 30

FRUIT SEEDS.

	Per oz.	Per lb.
Apple Seed		$0 60
Apricot Pits		10
Cherry Pits, Black Mazzard and Mahaleb		45
Currants, Cherry, Red Dutch and White Dutch	$0 40	
Gooseberry, Mixed	1 00	
Lemon	40	4 00
Orange, Tahiti	50	5 00
Peach Pits		10
Pear Seed	15	1 50
Plum Pits, Damson, Green Gage and Myrobolan		40
Quince Seed	20	2 00
Raspberry Seed	25	2 50
Strawberry, Large-fruited sorts, mixed	50	
Vitis riparia. This variety adapts itself to all climates and soils, and is, without doubt, the best resistant vine; it is strongly recommended by all French authorities, and has given success wherever it has been planted. Our supply has been collected from districts where this variety grows wild	30	3 00

BIRD SEEDS, POULTRY FOOD, ETC.

	1 lb.	100 lbs.
Bird Seed, Our Celebrated Mixture. Without doubt the cleanest and best mixture in the market, and the safest to use for pet birds . . . . In lb. boxes, 10 cts. each; in bulk,		$7 00
Bird Sand. Recleaned . . . . per box, 10 cts. .		
Bone Meal. For chickens		2 00
Canary. Best Sicily, recleaned	$0 10	7 00
Cuttle-Fish Bone	75	
Hemp	10	7 00
Manhattan Egg-Food . . . . 2-lb. package, 40 cts. .		
Morris' Poultry Cure . . . . 1-lb tins, 50 cts.; 2-lb. tins, 75 cts. .		
Maw Seed (*Blue Poppy*)	20	15 00
Millet	10	7 00
Oyster Shells. Ground		2 00
Rape	10	7 00
Rough Rice	15	10 00
Sunflower. For parrots	10	8 00

Grape-Dust is a Sure Cure for Mildew on Roses, etc.

MISCELLANEOUS AGRICULTURAL SEEDS, Etc.

	Lb.	100 lbs.
Beans, English Horse . . . . Market price for large quantity	$0 10	

JAPANESE BUCKWHEAT

NATURAL SIZE

Broom Corn, Improved Evergreen. This variety is extensively grown on account of the color and quality of its brush, which is long, fine, straight and always green . . . . — 10 — 58 00

Buckwheat, Japanese. Enormously prolific, yielding double the weight of the other varieties, and makes an excellent flour . . . . — 15 — 8 00

Buckwheat, Silver-Hull. Earlier than the preceding, and a good yielder; seed of a silvery gray color; flour white and nutritious . . . . . — 10 — 7 00

Caper Tree. This plant furnishes the Caper of commerce . . . . per pkt., 15 cts.; per oz., $1 .

Chufas or Earth Almond (*Cyperus æsculentus*). The nuts grow under ground near the surface; are sweet and nutritious food for pigs or poultry, who greedily eat them and take on firm fat from them. Fifteen pounds will plant an acre . . . . — 25

Egyptian Corn, Brown (*Millo Maize*). Produces a large quantity of forage, even under excessive drought; can be cut several times during the season, as it springs again freely from the root . . . . — 10 — 5 00

Egyptian Corn, White (*Dhoura or Guinea Corn*) — 10 — 4 00

Flax Seed. For sowing . . . . — 7 — 6 00

Flax Seed, Ground. For feeding . . . . — 8 — 7 00

Hop Seed . . . . per pkt., 10 cts.; per oz., 75 cts. . 10 00

Lupins. Blue, White and Yellow . . . . each, 35

Millets. The several varieties will be found under the head of Grass Seeds.

Peanut. The soil for this crop should be fertile, deep and mellow; plant in rows three and a-half feet apart, dropping peanuts at intervals of two feet, and covering them two or three inches; the yield, under proper culture, will exceed fifty bushels per acre . . . . Larger quantities at market prices . 15

	Lb.	100 lbs.
Sorghum, Early Amber. Grows eleven or twelve feet high and stands up well; the seed is highly relished by poultry and all kinds of stock	$0 10	$6 00
Sorghum, Early Orange. A popular variety in the south, and best adapted to that climate . . .	10	6 00
Sorghum Halapense. Known also as Evergreen Millet and Johnson Grass. Remarkable for its adaptability to all kinds of soil and climate; specially desirable where there is little rainfall, as it will thrive for months without moisture . .	20	15 00
Sunflower, Russian Mammoth. May be grown to advantage in waste pieces of ground, the seed being an excellent and cheap food for poultry	10	8 00
Tobacco, Connecticut Seed-Leaf. oz., 30 cts. .	2 50	
Tobacco, Imported Havana. The well-known excellent qualities of this variety render it indispensable . . . . per oz., 40 cts. .	4 00	
Vetches or Tares. Largely grown in England and Canada for stock. Generally mixed with oats and sown broadcast like wheat or barley, at the rate of eighty pounds per acre; cut when green, it makes excellent fodder	15	9 00

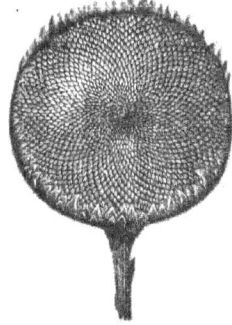

RUSSIAN MAMMOTH SUNFLOWER.

Whale-Oil Soap is a Cheap and Effective Insecticide.

TREE AND SHRUB SEEDS.

Amateur cultivators will please remember that the seeds of this class take time to germinate—in some cases only a few days, in others several weeks—and that quite frequently they lie dormant the whole season before commencing to grow.

We do not sell seeds of this class in quantities of less than an ounce of any one variety, except those that are quoted at over twenty-five cents per ounce; if these, twenty-five cent packets will be supplied.

	Per oz	Per lb
Abies brachyphylla. One of the hardiest and handsomest of Silver Firs	$0 60	$5 00
Abies concolor (*California White Silver Fir*). A very beautiful species	60	6 00
" excelsa (*Norway Spruce*). A well-known, lofty tree	15	75
" firma (*Japan Silver Fir*). Very hardy; graceful, pyramidal form	30	3 00
" macrocarpa. Resembles *Abies Douglasii*, and known as the Great-coned Spruce of California	60	6 00
" Mariesii. A Japanese variety of wondrous beauty	60	6 00
" Veitchii. A tall, handsome, slender variety from Japan	60	6 00
Acacia dealbata (*Silver Wattle*). Produces beautiful, yellow flowers	50	
" Drummondii. Very handsome dwarf shrub, with pale yellow flowers	60	
" lophantha (*Crested Wattle*). A graceful and highly ornamental variety	50	
Araucaria imbricata (*Monkey Puzzle*). A remarkable tree, with rigid, whorled branches, clothed with thick, hard, spine-tipped, imbricated leaves	75	
Acer glabrum (*Oregon Maple*). Grows from fifteen to thirty feet high	25	2 50
Ampelopsis Veitchii (*Japanese or Boston Ivy*). One of the best climbing plants there is; foliage changes to bright scarlet in the autumn	25	2 50
Amygdalis communis (*Bitter Almond*). Well-known ornamental flowering shrub	25	
Berberis aquifolium Californicum. Grows to a height of six or eight feet, and bears a profusion of yellow flowers	75	7 50
Betula pendula (*Weeping Birch*). The most popular of all weeping trees; the graceful, drooping branches and silvery white bark are attractive characteristics that are unsurpassed	30	3 00
Camellia Japonica. Well known flowering shrub	20	2 00
Castanea Japonica (*Japanese Chestnut*). A magnificent tree	10	1 00
Catalpa Kaempferi (*Japanese Catalpa*). Deep green, glossy foliage	25	2 50

	Per oz	Per lb
Citrus trifoliata. A hardy variety of ornamental orange from Japan	$0 25	$2 50
Cladrastis tinctoria (*Yellow Wood*). Hardy deciduous tree, bearing a great profusion of white flowers	75	7 00
Cornus Nuttallii (*Nuttall's Dogwood*). Large white flowers	25	2 50
Cryptomeria Japonica (*Japanese Cedar*). A fast-growing tree; forms handsome, conical specimens, fit to beautify any location	25	2 00
Cupressus Lawsoniana. One of the hardiest and most ornamental species of this genus, the slender, feathery branchlets being most elegant	40	4 00
Cupressus macrocarpa (*Monterey Cypress*). The most handsome and easily grown of all ornamental evergreen trees	15	1 25
Cytisus Laburnum (*Golden Chain*). Very ornamental; bright yellow flowers	15	75
Diospyros Kaki (*Japan Persimmon*). Produces excellent fruit	20	2 00
Eucalyptus globulus (*Tasmanian Blue Gum*). Splendid, fast-growing tree, valuable for its hygienic properties as well as for its timber	40	4 00

ABIES EXCELSA.

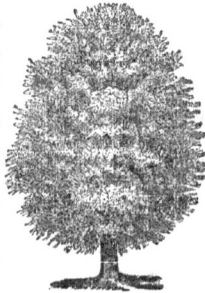

ACER GLABRUM

You can't get along well without one of the Rubber Sprinklers; see page 33.

TREE AND SHRUB SEEDS, Continued.

	Per oz.	Per lb.
Eucalyptus ficifolia.. A magnificent crimson-flowered variety . . . . . . Per 100 seeds, $2 .		
Euonymus Europaea. The European Burning Bush.	$0 25	$2 00
Fremontia Californica. A hardy deciduous shrub; produces a profusion of bright yellow flowers . . .	75	
Genista scoparia (*Scotch Broom*). Beautiful yellow flowers	10	75
Gleditschia triacanthos (*Honey Locust*). Handsome, tall tree	10	60
" **Japonica** (*Japanese Honey Locust*) . .	25	2 50
Gymnocladus Canadensis (*Kentucky Coffee Tree*). Rapid grower, with fine, feathery foliage	15	1 00
Hamamelis Japonica (*Japanese Witch Hazel*) . . .	30	3 00
Hedera Helix (*English Ivy*)	20	2 00
Juglans nigra (*Black Walnut*).		20
" **Sieboldii** (*Japanese Walnut*)	10	75
Larix Europea. An elegant and rapid-growing pyramidal tree	20	1 00
Libocedrus decurrens. Known as the *White Cedar of California*; fine, hardy timber tree	40	4 00
Ligustrum Japonicum (*Japan Privet*). A robustgrowing, evergreen shrub; white flowers, slightly fragrant	20	2 00
Magnolia grandiflora. A magnificent evergreen with stately form, producing a profusion of exquisitely fragrant flowers	30	3 00
Myrica Californica. The Bay Berry or Wax Myrtle of California	50	5 00
Oreodaphne Californica (*California Sassafras*). Evergreen shrub, emitting a strong odor of camphor	25	2 00
Photinia arbutifolia (*Madrono Tree*). A very handsome shrub; flowers white; bark of the young wood bright red	20	2 00
Picea grandis (*Balsam Fir*). Grows rapidly in rich, moist soils; a valuable timber tree	40	4 00
" **nobilis** (*California Red Fir*). A magnificent tree, making fine timber, which is said to be better than that of other firs	50	5 00
" **polita.** A beautiful tree, called by the Japanese the "Tiger's Tail Fir."	75	7 50
Pinus Coulteri. Handsome and distinct species	30	3 00
" **densiflora.** A rapid-growing, beautiful, hardy species from Japan	40	4 00
" **Koraiensis.** An elegant, small, compact-growing variety from Japan	75	7 50
" **Lambertiana.** A tall, massive variety of elegant appearance	30	3 00
" **monophylla.** A small, slow-growing species, with dense, bushy head	30	3 00
" **Parryana.** A very large tree, the bark of which is divided into large, flat, smooth plates . .	40	4 00
" **parviflora.** A distinct, small-growing species, with dense foliage	50	5 00
" **ponderosa** (*Yellow Pine*). One of the largest pines known; found at a very high elevation, consequently very hardy	40	4 00
" **Sabiniana** (*Nut Pine*). Small and spreading habit	30	3 00
" **Torreyana.** Tall and graceful, with tufted foliage	30	3 00
Quercus crysolepis.		
" **dumosa.**		
" **Englemanni.** Four varieties of Oaks, natives of California; ornamental, and worthy of a place in every collection.	40	4 00
" **Kellogii.**		
Rhamnus Californicus (*California Buckthorn*).	50	5 00
Ribes bracteosum (*California Black Currant*).	75	7 50
Robinia pseudacacia (*Yellow Locust*)	10	50
Rosa canina (*Dog Rose*)	10	50
" **rugosa.** A beautiful hardy variety from Japan	50	5 00
" **rubiginosa** (*Sweet Briar*). A favorite old variety	15	1 50
Salisburia adiantifolia (*Maiden Hair Tree*). A native of Japan; of rapid growth and beautiful, fern-like foliage	15	1 00
Schinus Molle (*Pepper Tree*). A well-known tree, with handsome fern-like, drooping foliage . . .	15	1 00
Sequoia gigantea (*Wellingtonia gigantea*). The Mammoth Tree of California; the largest tree known to exist on the American Continent	75	7 50

CUPRESSUS LAWSONIANA. (See page 30.)

If you want a good Lawn, read page 2.

TREE AND SHRUB SEEDS, Continued.

	Per oz.	Per lb
Sequoia sempervirens (*California Red Wood*). Next in size to the preceding, and the most valuable tree of the California forests	$0 40	$4 00
Spiræa ariæfolia (*California Spiræa*)	50	5 00
Syringa Japonica (*Japan Lilac*). A new, large-foliaged variety from Japan	1 00	12 00
Thuja aurea (*Golden Arbor-Vitæ*). An elegant shrub, with dense, flat, green foliage, tinged with yellow	30	3 00
" occidentalis (*American Arbor-Vitæ*). A beautiful native tree, especially valuable for screens and hedges	25	2 50
" gigantea. The Giant Arbor-Vitæ of Oregon	50	5 00
Thuyopsis dolobrata (*Japanese Thuja*). A beautiful pyramidal tree	60	6 00
Tilia Europea (*European Linden*)	10	75
Wistaria Sinensis. A magnificent climbing shrub	40	4 00
" " alba. A white variety of the preceding ; very desirable	60	6 00
Yucca baccata. Very effective in sub-tropical gardening	75	
" Whipplei. A native of California and Arizona	50	

INSECTICIDES.

Fir Tree Oil. The best insecticide for indoor use on all plants ; is also a valuable remedy for animal parasites and insects. Per pint, $1.

Grape Dust. (*Hammond's.*) A non-poisonous powder for the remedy of mildew and rot on grapes, gooseberries, roses, etc. Per 5-lb. package, 40 cts.; per barrel in bulk, price on application.

Hellebore. Powdered white hellebore, for the destruction of caterpillars, slugs, worms, etc. Per lb., 40 cts.

Ongerth's Insecticide Powder No. 1. This powder kills or drives away all vermin and insects injurious to vegetable and animal life, such as slugs, snails, ants, fleas, lice, caterpillars, etc., etc. 1-lb., sprinkle-top cans, 50 cents ; 4-lb. cans, $1.

Paris Green. Largely used for the destruction of potato bugs, caterpillars, worms, etc.; being deadly poison, great caution is necessary when using it. Per lb., 35 cts.

Slug Shot. (*Hammond's.*) A cheap, popular and effective insecticide, easily applied and not injurious or dangerous to animals. 5-lb. package, 40 cts.; per barrel in bulk, price on application.

Tobacco Soap. Easy of application, and fatal to all insect life, whether on plants or animals. Per 8-oz. tin, 25 cts.; per 6-oz. tin, 20 cts.

Tobacco Stems. Indispensable for the fumigation of greenhouses, etc., and for the destruction of black aphis, green fly and other insects. Per bale of about 250 lbs., $3.50.

Whale Oil Soap. Excellent wash for trees and plants to prevent insects from lodging in the bark, and for smearing on the trunks of trees to prevent worms from crawling up. Per 1-lb. tin, 20 cts.; in bulk in quantities of 10 lbs. and over, 10 cents per pound.

INSECTICIDE DISTRIBUTORS.

The "Stott" Distributor. A cylinder or oblong machine separated by means of perforated divisions into cells. Into these cells the manure or insecticide, in solid or liquid form, is inserted. At each end of the machine is a length of tubing, one end being attached to the water-tap or garden-pump, and the other to an ordinary hose-pipe, the water being forced through, and consequently impregnated with the composition. Price, including filler and hose-coupling, copper : 2 cells, $9 ; 3 cells, $10 ; 5 cells, $12.

The "Stott" Patent Sprayer. This sprayer gives a spray resembling a mist, and for insecticide purposes is perfect, as it enables the operator not only to get under the leaves, but to spray every part of the plant in the most perfect manner. Having but one opening, it possesses the rare and very important advantage of never becoming clogged. Price, $1.

Order now ; don't wait until you are going to plant.

FERTILIZERS.

We supply only high-grade reliable fertilizers, goods that we know to be as represented; and, quality considered, prices are unusually low.

	Per 100 lbs.	Per ton.
Ground Bone	$2 50	$35 00
Pure Guano Flour. Guaranteed to contain 48 to 50 per cent. bone phosphate (the same as pure bone-meal) and 1½ per cent. ammonia	2 25	30 00
Plain Superphosphate. Or dissolved guano (guano treated with sulphuric acid), containing about 16 per cent. available phosphoric acid and 1 per cent. ammonia	2 50	40 00
Brand A. Guaranteed to contain 10 to 11 per cent. phosphoric acid, 9 to 10 per cent. potash, 3 to 4 per cent. ammonia; specially adapted for sugar cane	3 00	50 00
Brand B. Guaranteed to contain 14 to 15 per cent. phosphoric acid, 2 per cent. potash, 2 per cent. ammonia; adapted for grain crops and general use	2 75	45 00
Brand C. Guaranteed to contain 12 per cent. phosphoric acid, 5 to 6 per cent. potash, 3 to 4 per cent. ammonia, suitable for grass	3 00	47 50
Brand D. Or nitrated superphosphate, a very high grade, intended for irrigated fruit orchards where the soil and irrigating water are found rich in potash. Contains 15 per cent. phosphoric acid (nearly all available) and 3½ per cent. ammonia	2 75	43 00
Gypsum or Land Plaster	1 75	22 50

MISCELLANEOUS HORTICULTURAL REQUISITES

	Each
Atomizers. (Woodason's Bellows.) Convenient for the application of liquid insecticides	$2 00
Bellows. Woodason's Powder for Hellebore, Tobacco Dust, etc.	$1, $2 and 3 00
Fertilizers. See above.	
Forks. Digging or Spading	$1 to 1 50
Garden Lines. Finest Braided, 100 feet length	75
Garden Reels. To hold garden lines	75
Grafting Wax. In ¼, ½ and lb. packages	per lb., 50 cents
Hoes. Draw or Corn	60 cents to 75
Hose Menders. For repairing rubber hose. See page 2.	
Hose, Rubber. Several sizes and qualities. See page 2.	
Insecticides. See page 32.	
Knives, Budding. Best English makes; ivory handles	$1 to 2 00
Knives, Pruning. Best English makes	75 cents to 1 50

Labels. Plant and Tree, Wooden Painted—

	4½-inch	5-inch	6-inch	8-inch	3½-inch tree.
Price { Per hundred	$0 30	$0 35	$0 40	$0 60	$0 25
Per thousand	1 25	1 40	1 50	5 00	1 15

Lawn Mowers. Send for special circular.	
Mole Traps, Olmsted's Improved	2 00
Moss. Sphagnum for florists' use, packing, etc	in 100 lb. bales, $6; per lb., 15 cents.
Peat. For Orchids and other plants	per 100 lbs., $8; per lb., 10 cents.

Plant Sticks. Painted green—

	3 feet	4 feet	5 feet	6 feet
Price { Per dozen	$1 00	$1 25	$1 50	$2 00
Per hundred	7 00	8 00	10 00	12 00

Raffia. For tying plants; superior to twine	per lb., 25 cents; 5 lbs. for $1.
Rakes. Steel Garden; handled	40 to 80
Saws. Pruning; double edged	75 cents to 1 25
Scissors. Grape; for thinning the bunches	$1 to 1 50
Scythes. English lawn; in sizes	$1 50 to 2 00
Scythe Stones. Round Welsh Talacre	per dozen, $2 . 20
Shears. Hand Pruning; solid steel	$1 50 to 3 00
Shovels. Ames' best cast steel; square and diamond-pointed	$1 25 to 1 50
Spades. Best quality, long or short handle	$1 25 to 1 50
Sprinklers, Rubber. For sprinkling cut-flowers, seedlings, clothes, etc.	1 25
Syringes. Brass; of superior manufacture, highly finished	$2 to 6 00
Trowels. Solid steel, welded extra strong	50
Weeders. Excelsior Hand; a useful article around plants	25

Fertilizer, "Brand C," is a great grass invigorator.

"Planet Jr." Horse and Hand Implements

For many years these have been recognized as the most popular and satisfactory tools made for garden and farm use, and to-day the trade-mark "Planet Jr." is the synonym for excellence the world over. In this space we can only partially describe a few of the best, but if readers are interested, a special list will be mailed them on application.

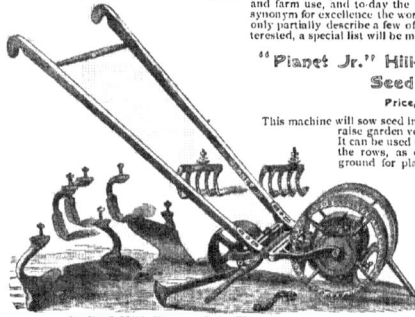

"Planet Jr." Hill-Dropping Garden-Seed Drill.

Price, $12.

This machine will sow seed in hills, and is the best for all who raise garden vegetables on an extensive scale. It can be used to straddle the row, or between the rows, as desired. The rakes level the ground for planting, gather stones and trash, cultivate, cover seed, etc. The hoes cut loose and clean, killing everything they meet, leaving the ground level. The cultivator teeth mellow the soil deep or shallow, and are useful for marking out. The plows lay out deep furrows and cover them, hill up or plow away, as desired. The leaf-guards allow cultivation of large plants, such as beets, carrots, parsnips, beans and peas. No vegetable grower can afford to be without it. It will do very efficiently an amount

COMBINED DRILL, WHEEL-HOE, CULTIVATOR, RAKE AND PLOW.

of work equal to that of six men with ordinary hand-hoes. Weight, packed, 44 pounds.

"Planet Jr." Combined Hill-Dropping Seed and Fertilizer Drill.

Price, $18.

This machine is exactly the same as the above, with the addition of a fertilizer hopper. The fertilizer can be sown either above or below the seed, as desired, by setting that plow deeper or shallower than the other. This machine will be a great boon to all farmers and market-gardeners. It is thoroughly well-made, and guaranteed to do satisfactory work. Weight, packed, 58 pounds.

"Planet Jr." Combined Drill, Wheel-Hoe, Cultivator, Rake and Plow

Price, $12.

This is the most popular and perfect machine of its kind made. All blades are steel, tempered and polished. The rakes are invaluable in preparing the ground for planting, for covering seeds, first cultivation, etc. The hoes work closely and safely all rows up to sixteen inches wide at one passage, leaving the ground nearly level. The plow opens furrows, covers them, hills, plows to and from, etc. The cultivator teeth are admirably adapted to deep mellowing of the soil and marking out. Taken as a whole, this combined tool is the nearest approach to perfection for the uses of a gardener that can well be devised in a single implement. Weight, packed, 40 pounds.

"Planet Jr." Double-Wheel Hoe, Cultivator, Rake and Plow.

Price, $8.

This implement is a great favorite, especially for field work. Hoes both sides of the row at once, at the speed of a moderate walk. Careful practice will enable any one to become skillful in a short time, the chief rule being to watch the wheels only, keeping them at the proper distance from the row. The tools follow the wheels accurately, and the whole operation in a short time becomes easy, rapid and pleasant. The leaf-guards in front are just the thing needed when hoeing large plants, such as beets, parsnips, carrots, beans and peas, enabling you to cultivate them perfectly, when otherwise the leaves would be torn off and the plants seriously injured. Weight, packed, 35 pounds.

Other "Planet Jr." Implements.

	Price.
Single-Wheel Hoe, Cultivator, Rake and Plow. Weight, packed, 26 pounds	$6 00
Fire-Fly Hand-Plow. Weight, packed, 12 pounds	2 50
Market-Gardener's Horse-Hoe, Complete. Weight, packed, 70 pounds	12 50

Handsomely Illustrated and Descriptive Catalogues of "Planet Jr." Implements Mailed Free on Application.

"The Refinement and Happiness of a Home can be Measured by the Flowers Around It."

GENERAL LIST OF

Select Flower Seeds.

ANNUALS grow, bloom and die the first year from seed. **BIENNIALS** bloom the second year from seed, and then die ; though many, if sown early in the spring, will flower the first year. **PERENNIALS** usually bloom the second year from seed, and continue to grow and bloom for many years ; some will also bloom the first year, if sown early.

☞ All Flower Seeds sent free by mail on receipt of price. Full cultural directions on each packet.

ABUTILON.

A well-known, showy plant, with beautiful, bell-shaped flowers of various bright colors.

Choice Mixed. 10 cents per pkt.

ACACIA.

Graceful, elegant and highly ornamental shrubs, their fine foliage and habit never failing to attract attention.

Choice Mixed. 10 cents per pkt.

AGERATUM.

Useful for ribbon borders or masses, and also for cutting for the use of the florist, etc.

AMARANTHUS TRICOLOR.

Mexicanum. Blue. 5 cents per pkt.
   " Album. White. 5 cents per pkt.

ALYSSUM.

Free-flowering, useful, pretty little plants for beds, edgings or rockwork.

Odoratum. White, very sweet. 5 cents per pkt.
   " Compactum. Quite distinct, charming annual. 10 cents per pkt.

AQUILEGIA. (Columbine.)

A class of highly ornamental plants, with curiously formed flowers of striking and beautiful colors.

Mixed. 5 cents per pkt.

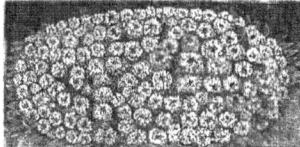

ALYSSUM.

AMARANTHUS.

Peculiarly valuable on account of the great beauty of the foliage, which is handsomely formed and highly colored.

Caudatus (Loves-Lies-Bleeding). 5 cents per pkt.
Salicifolius (Fountain Plant). 5 cents per pkt.
   Tricolor (Joseph's Coat). 5 cents per pkt.
   Fine Mixed. cents per pkt.

SNAPDRAGON.

ANTIRRHINUM. (Snapdragon.)

A showy and useful perennial, bearing very beautiful spikes of gay colored flowers ; it amply repays the labor of cultivation, and should have a place in every garden.

Tom Thumb. Mixed ; very compact grower. 5 cents per pkt.

AURICULA.

A garden favorite of great beauty, and of rapidly increasing popularity ; succeeds best in a northern aspect.

Choice Mixed. Carefully saved from selected flowers of finest form and richest colors. 25 cents per pkt.

One Trial will convince you that "QUALITY" is Our Motto.

QUILLED GERMAN ASTER.

ASTERS.

This is not only one of the most popular, but one of the most effective of our garden favorites, producing in profusion flowers in which richness and variety of color are combined with the most perfect and beautiful form. Every one of the following classes possesses some distinguishing merit, and we have restricted the colors to those which are distinct and certain to please.

Bouquet. Mixed colors. 10 cents per pkt.
    "   **White.** Compact and free-flowering. 10 cents per pkt.
Chrysanthemum-flowered. Brilliant colors mixed. 10 cents per pkt.
Cockade or Crown. Mixed colors. 10 cts. per pkt.
Mignon. A new class resembling the Victoria, but more floriferous; pure white. 25 cents per pkt.
Quilled German. Mixed colors. 5 cents per pkt.
Rose-flowered. Mixed colors. 10 cents per pkt.
Shakespeare. Very dwarf; mixed colors. 10 cents per pkt.
Truffaut's Peony Perfection. One of the finest Asters cultivated; large fine flowers, with long, beautifully incurved petals. Brilliant colors; mixed. 10 cents per pkt.
Truffaut's Crimson. 15 cents per pkt.
    "   **White.** 15 cents per pkt.
Victoria. Mixed colors. 10 cents per pkt.
Washington. Mixed colors. 10 cents per pkt.
    Choice Mixed. Our own growing; brightest and best colors only. 50 cents per oz.; 5 cents per pkt.

BALLOON VINE.

Ornamental, rapid growing climber, remarkable chiefly as having an inflated membranous capsule, from which it derives its common name.

Cardiospermum halicacabum. 5 cents per pkt.

BALLOON VINE.

BALSAMS.

Magnificent plants, producing gorgeous masses of beautiful brilliant colored flowers in great profusion.

Alabaster. The grandest white variety grown. 15 cents per pkt.
Blood Red. 10 cents per pkt.
Blush. Delicate rosy pink. 10 cents per pkt.
Peach Blossom. 10 cents per pkt.
Primrose. Beautiful citron-yellow. 10 cts. per pkt.
Mixed Double. 5 cents per pkt.

BELLIS. (English Daisy.)

A well-known popular favorite for garden or pot culture; very free in bloom.

Longfellow. Beautiful rose. 15 cents per pkt.
Snowball. Pure white. 15 cents per pkt.
Choice Mixed. 10 cents per pkt.

BALSAMS.

BRACHYCOME.

Beautiful free-flowering plants, covered with a profusion of Cineraria-like flowers; very effective for edgings.
Iberidifolia. Blue Swan River Daisy. 5 cents per pkt.

BROWALLIA.

Exceedingly pretty plants for bedding purposes, furnishing an abundance of strikingly beautiful flowers.
Elata. Blue. 5 cents per pkt.

CALCEOLARIA.

The strain of this magnificent flower that we offer is obtained from a celebrated English grower, and for variety and brilliancy of color has no superior
Hybrida Grandiflora. 25 cents per pkt.

We can Guarantee Satisfaction, because we Know what we Sell.

CALENDULA.

Showy, free-flowering plants, deserving a place in every garden.

Meteor. Beautifully striped orange and yellow. 5 cents per pkt.
Queen of Trianon. Bright canary-yellow, with maroon center. 10 cts. per pkt.

CALLA.
(Richardia.)

A handsome, easily grown old favorite; thrives in any light, rich soil, when plentifully watered.

Æthiopica. 10 cents per pkt.

CAMELLIA.

Specially saved for us from a large collection

CANDYTUFT.

of the choicest sorts in Japan; of superior quality. The seeds often lie dormant for many weeks.

Japonica. 15 cents per pkt.

CANDYTUFT.

One of the most useful and effective annuals we have; indispensable for bouquets.

Crimson. Very dark. 5 cents per pkt.
Empress. A new large-flowered, pure white variety. 10 cents per pkt.
Mixed. All colors. 5 cents per pkt.

MARGARET CARNATION.

CANNA.

For list of choice named varieties, see third page of cover. Handsome foliage plants, that make an imposing display in any location.
Crozy's Mixed. 10 cents per pkt.

CARNATION.

A magnificent class of popular favorites, that stand unrivalled for delicacy of markings and delicious fragrance.
Choice Mixed. 25 cents per pkt.
Early Grenadin. Salmon red; very fine. 15 cents per pkt.
Margaret. Especially adapted for pot-culture. 25 cents per pkt.
Perpetual or Tree. 25 cents per pkt.
Vienna Dwarf. Double, sweet-scented flowers, in a great variety of colors. 10 cents per pkt.

ANNUAL CHRYSANTHEMUM.

CENTAUREA.

An interesting genus, remarkable for the free-flowering habit of some of its members, and the beautiful, silvery foliage of others.
Cyanus (Bachelor's Button). Mixed. 5 cts. per pkt.
Gymnocarpa (Dusty Miller). Silvery foliage. 10 cents per pkt.

CHRYSANTHEMUM.

Well-known plants, remarkable for diversity of form and color. The seed we offer was specially saved for us in Japan.

Superb Mixed. 15 cents per pkt.
Eclipse. An easily grown, annual sort; pure golden yellow, with a scarlet ring on the ray of the florets, the disk being dark brown. 10 cents per pkt.
Marguerite or Paris Daisy. White, star-shaped flowers. 5 cents per pkt.

Have You Tried the Menlo Park Pansies? You Ought To !

COBÆA SCANDENS.

COBÆA SCANDENS.

A rapid and graceful climber, with large, bell-shaped, dark blue flowers ; very handsome foliage. 10 cents per pkt.

CLARKIA.

Charming plant for borders, growing freely and blossoming profusely in almost any common garden soil

Elegans alba.   Pure white.   5 cents per pkt.
    "   Salmon Queen.   Pink.   5 cents per pkt.
Fine Mixed.   5 cents per pkt

CLIANTHUS DAMPIERII.

One of the most magnificent flowers in cultivation, with singularly beautiful foliage and magnificent clusters of large, scarlet, pea-shaped flowers, picturesquely marked with a black blotch   25 cents per pkt

COSMOS.

CONVOLVULUS.

The well-known "Morning Glory," so popular that it needs no description. The dwarf varieties are excellent for vases, etc.

Major.   Mixed colors.   5 cents per pkt.
Minor.   Mixed colors.   5 cents per pkt.

COSMOS.

One of the most showy and graceful of all annuals; grows from five to six feet high, and is covered with large, single, dahlia-like flowers of every shade of color.

Pure White.   15 cents per pkt.
Mixed colors.   10 cents per pkt.

CINERARIA.

Very showy plants; profuse bloomers, and elegant for conservatory decoration; flowers of rich coloring.
Hybrida grandiflora.   25 cents per pkt.

CINERARIA.

COCKSCOMB. (Celosia.)

Handsome, free-blooming plants of easy culture, producing pretty flowers in combs and feathery spikes.
Cristata nana.   "Glasgow Prize."   Distinct dwarf variety, with dark foliage and crimson combs.   10 cents per pkt.
Japonica.   Very showy and distinct.   10 cts per pkt.
Plumosa.   Mixed   5 cents per pkt.

COLEUS.

Ornamental-leaved plants, largely used for bedding purposes ; easily raised from seed.
Choice Mixed.   10 cents per pkt.

Our Collections of Flower Seeds (Page 2 of the Cover) are Wonderfully Fine.

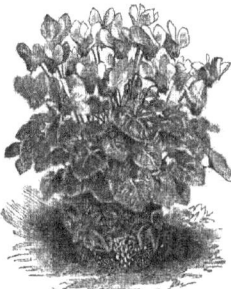

CYCLAMEN PERSICUM.

COLLINSIA.

Free-flowering annuals of great beauty, and well worth a place in every garden.

Fine Mixed. 5 cents per pkt.

CYCLAMEN.

Deservedly admired, and as plants for pot-culture have no rivals. Flowering bulbs can be had from seed in one year. The strain we offer produces flowers of extraordinary size and great substance, with large foliage, beautifully marked with silver-gray.

Giganteum. Mixed. 50 cents per pkt.
Persicum. Mixed. 25 cents per pkt.

CYPRESS VINE.

The vines have delicate, Fern-like foliage, and beautiful, star-like flowers borne in clusters; splendid climbers.

Scarlet. 5 cents per pkt.
White. 5 cents per pkt.
Mixed. All colors of this fine climber. 5 cts. per pkt.

DAHLIA.

These flower freely the first year from seed, giving as good if not better results than the bulbs. The single varieties are exceedingly handsome, both as to form and colors.

Double. Choice mixed. 15 cts. per pkt.
Single. Fine mixed. 10 cts. per pkt.

SINGLE DAHLIA.

DELPHINIUM. (Larkspur.)

Handsome, and much prized for the rich color of the flowers; the perennial sorts are well adapted for permanent locations.

Perennial varieties. Mixed. 10 cents per pkt.
Annual Varieties. Mixed. 5 cents per pkt.

DAISY, ENGLISH.

See *Bellis.*

DIANTHUS. (Pinks.)

Of immense value for bedding purposes, as the flowers retain their beauty during the entire summer.

DIANTHUS.

The colors are marvelous, ranging from pure white to richest crimson, and beautifully laced and striped.

Chinensis. Double; mixed colors. 5 cents per pkt.
Heddewegii. Double; mixed colors. 10 cts. per pkt.
Laciniatus. Beautifully fringed. 10 cents per pkt.
Imperialis. Double; mixed colors. 5 cents per pkt.

DIGITALIS. (Foxglove.)

Ornamental, showy perennials for shrubberies or other shady locations; flowers borne in dense spikes.

Gloxinoides. Best colors mixed. 5 cents per pkt.

ESCHSCHOLTZIA
(California Poppy.)

An exceedingly showy class of plants, bearing a profusion of richly-colored flowers; attractive for bed-

DIGITALIS.

ding, massing, etc., giving fine effects.

Californica. Pale yellow. 5 cents per pkt.
Crocea alba. Pure white. 5 cents per pkt.
Rose Cardinal. Showy, rose-colored flowers. 10 cents per pkt.
Mixed. 5 cents per pkt.

EVERLASTING FLOWERS.

The following is a selection of the very best varieties of this class. They are highly prized as an ornament to the garden when growing, and for the winter decoration of vases, etc., they have no superior.

Acroclinium. Mixed, Rose and White. 5 cts. per pkt.
Gomphrena. Mixed. (*Bachelor's Buttons.*) 5 cents per pkt.
Helichrysum. Dwarf varieties mixed. 5 cents per pkt.
Rhodanthe. Mixed. 5 cents per pkt.
Xeranthemum. Mixed. 5 cents per pkt.
Mixed Everlastings. Many varieties other than above. 5 cents per pkt.

ESCHSCHOLTZIA.

Read what we say about Cannas, third page of Cover.

MYOSOTIS.

FORGET-ME-NOT. (Myosotis.)

These modest little flowers are greatly prized, and succeed well in moderately moist locations. *Myosotis Palustris* is the true "Forget-Me-Not" of Europe.

Alpestris. Blue. 5 cents per pkt.
Dissitiflora. Flowers very early; blue. 10 cents per pkt.
Palustris semperflorens. Beautiful blue. 10 cents per pkt.
Sylvatica alba. Pure white. 10 cents per pkt.

FREESIA REFRACTA ALBA.

The delicate creamy tints and delicious perfume of this flower have made it immensely popular, and when it is remembered that within six months from sowing the seed you can possess flowers that are perfect gems, the great hold it has on public favor will not be wondered at. 10 cents per pkt.

FUCHSIA.

This well-known plant is much more easily cultivated

from seed than is generally supposed. They are of very robust habit, and bloom profusely within six months from the time of sowing. The seed we offer has been carefully saved from the choicest double and single varieties, and will produce a large proportion of most desirable sorts.

Superb Mixed. 25 cents per pkt.

FUCHSIA.

FOUR O'CLOCKS.

Known also as "Marvel of Peru." Beautiful annuals, bearing throughout the summer myriads of many-colored flowers.

Mixed Colors. 5 cents per pkt.

GAILLARDIA.

Remain long in flower, producing an abundance of bloom of fascinating color.

Grandiflora. Crimson, yellow and brown. 5 cents per pkt.
Lorenziana. Double; bright yellow and red. 5 cents per pkt.
Mixed Colors. 5 cents per pkt.

GILLIA.

The flowers are borne in great abundance, and make up well in bouquets, etc. Useful also for vases and rock-work.

Mixed Colors. 5 cents per pkt.

GODETIA.

Splendid, free-flowering annual, with large heads of cup-shaped flowers, remaining in bloom for a long time.

Duchess of Albany. Pure white. 5 cents per pkt.
Lady Albemarle. Bright crimson. 5 cents per pkt.
Mixed. 5 cents per pkt.

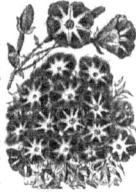

GODETIA.

GOURDS.

All of this class are highly interesting, principally on account of their peculiar fruits, both as regards shape and markings.

Bottle. Ornamental and useful. 5 cents per pkt.
Egg-shaped. 5 cents per pkt.
Hercules Club. 10 cents per pkt.
Orange. 5 cents per pkt.
Pear-shaped. 5 cents per pkt.
Mixed. Many curious varieties. 5 cents per pkt.

HELIOTROPE.

Favorite plants for bedding and pot-culture; much prised on account of their delicious fragrance.

Choice Mixed. 10 cts. pkt.

GOURDS.

HOLLYHOCK.

Can be grown from seed with the greatest ease; plants raised in this manner have proved far more robust than those grown from cuttings.

Canary Yellow. 10 cents per pkt.
Crimson. 10 cents per pkt.
Lavender. 10 cts. per pkt.
Rose. 10 cents per pkt.
White. 10 cents per pkt.
Above Colors Mixed. 10 cents per pkt.

Twenty-one superb varieties Sweet Peas, only $1.50; see Fourth page of Cover.

PAMPAS GRASS.

GRASSES, ORNAMENTAL.

The following are the most attractive and ornamental varieties, and for use in winter bouquets are indispensable :

Agrostis nebulosa. Very graceful. 5 cents per pkt.
Avena sterilis (Animated Oats). 5 cents per pkt.
Briza gracilis (Quaking Grass). 5 cents per pkt.
Coix lachryma (Job's Tears). 5 cents per pkt.
Eragrostis elegans (Love-grass). 5 cents per pkt.
Gynerium argenteum (Pampas Grass). 5 cents per pkt.
Stipa pennata (Feather Grass). 10 cents per pkt.
Mixed. Many kinds, other than the above. 5 cents per pkt.

HYACINTH BEAN. (Dolichos.)

A beautiful, quick-growing climber, with blue and white flowers borne in immense clusters ; very showy.

Lablab. Mixed. 5 cents per pkt.

IPOMŒA.

Elegant climbing plants with handsome, showy flowers and beautiful foliage. They are closely allied to and much like Morning Glory, and of tall and rapid growth.

MOON FLOWER (IPOMŒA).

Bona Nox (Evening Glory). Large violet flowers. 10 cts. per pkt.
Coccinea. Small, bright scarlet flowers. 5 cents per pkt.
Hederacea grandiflora. Ivy-leaved. 5 cents per pkt.
Mexicana hybrida alba (True Moon Flower). 10 cents per pkt.
Quamoclit. (See Cypress vine.)
Rubra Cœrulea. 10 cts. per pkt.
Mixed. Many varieties. 5 cents per pkt.

ICE PLANT.

A pretty trailing plant, the leaves of which are covered with crystalline globules ; very effective for rockwork and vases.

Mesembryanthemum crystallinum. 5 cents per pkt.

LANTANA.

Rapid growing, constant blooming perennials, suitable either for garden decoration or pot-culture.

Mixed. Orange, White and Pink. 10 cents per pkt.

LINARIA CYMBALARIA.

Beautiful, delicate trailer for baskets and vases, neat foliage and small blue flowers. Known as Kenilworth and Coliseum Ivy. 10 cents per pkt.

LINUM RUBRUM. (Scarlet Flax.)

A beautiful annual with dazzling scarlet flowers, delicate stems and fine foliage. One of the most effective and showy annuals grown. 5 cents per pkt.

LOBELIA.

For decorative purposes, such as vases, hanging baskets, borders of beds, etc., this graceful little plant is unsurpassed. All the varieties are very dwarf and compact, and form dense balls of flowers.

Crystal Palace. The finest blue. 10 cents per pkt.
Gracilis. Best for hanging baskets, etc. 10 cents per pkt.
Cardinalis. A scarlet, perennial sort ; very showy. 10 cents per pkt.

MAURANDIA BARCLAYANA.

Charming climber, elegant alike in flower and foliage, and of graceful, slender growth. Pale blue, pretty flower. 10 cents per pkt.

LANTANAS.

Try a Packet of our Perpetual-flowering Pelargoniums.

MARIGOLD.

MARIGOLD.

Very popular plants, producing a wealth of color throughout the season. The African varieties are self-colored, and the French are beautifully striped and spotted.

African. Mixed. 5 cents per pkt.
French. Mixed. 5 cents per pkt.

MIGNONETTE.

This fine old favorite has been greatly improved within recent years; below we offer the very best varieties for either pot or garden culture.

MIGNONETTE.

Bird's Mammoth. Immense spikes; distinct. 10 cts. per pkt.
Golden Queen. Very fragrant. 10 cents per pkt.
Grandiflora. Large and free-flowering. 5 cents per pkt.
Machet. The best for pot-culture. 10 cents per pkt.
Miles' Spiral. Splendid long spikes; one of the very best varieties, and under careful culture attains large size. 5 cents per pkt.
Sweet. Small flowered but very fragrant. 5c. per pkt.

MIMULUS. (Monkey Flower.)

MIMULUS.

Beautiful, singularly shaped and brilliantly colored flowers, with curious and various colored markings; do well in shady situations.

Hybrida. Many colors mixed. 10 cents per pkt.
Moschatus. The well-known Musk Plant. 10 cts per pkt.

MOONFLOWER.

See *Ipomœa Mexicana hybrida alba*, page 41.

MOMORDICA.

Curious plants, with ornamental foliage; the fruit is golden yellow, warted, and when ripe, opens, disclosing the seeds and brilliant interior; the whole fruit is valuable for medicinal purposes.

MOMORDICA.

Balsamina (Balsam Apple). 5 cents per pkt.
Charantia (Balsam Pear) 5 cents per pkt.

NASTURTIUM.

Tom Thumb or Dwarf Varieties.

These are indispensable for garden decoration, as they bloom profusely in any soil for a long period; they do better in poor rather than rich soil, and make a splendid bed on the lawn.

Crimson. 5 cents per pkt.
Crystal Palace Gem. Yellow, finely blotched with maroon. 5 cents per pkt.
Empress of India. Crimson-scarlet, with fine dark foliage. 5 cents per pkt.
Pearl. Creamy white. 5 cents per pkt.
Rose. Soft pink. 5 cents per pkt.
Mixed. 5 cents per pkt.

Tall Varieties.

These are splendid summer climbers.

Crimson. 5 cents per pkt.
Lobbianum ("Spit-Fire"). Brilliant scarlet. 10 cents per pkt.
Pearl. Creamy white. 5 cents per pkt.
Scarlet. 5 cents per pkt.
Shillingii. Orange, spotted. 10 cents per pkt.
Mixed. 5 cents per pkt.

NICOTIANA AFFINIS.

Deliciously fragrant, large white flowers; very ornamental. 10 cents per pkt.

DWARF NASTURTIUMS.

Our Fancy Caladiums are Marvels of Beauty.

PANSY, MENLO PARK STRAIN.

PANSY.

We are positive that the stocks that we have secured of this universal favorite are unsurpassed. Our "Menlo Park Strain" is perfection, and for variety of colors and size and texture of bloom it stands alone.

Azure Blue. Very fine. 5 cents per pkt.
Canary. Pale yellow. 5 cents per pkt
Emperor William. Ultramarine blue, with purple eye. 5 cents per pkt.
Faust. Black. 5 cents per pkt.
Lord Beaconsfield. Indigo, shading to pure white. 5 cents per pkt
Odier or Five-Spotted. 10 cents per pkt.
Snow Queen. Pure white. 5 cents per pkt
Menlo Park Mixed. Saved from our magnificent collection, and is the best sold. 25 cents per pkt.
Mixed. As usually sold. 5 cents per pkt.

PASSIFLORA. (Passion Flower.)

Rapid-growing climbers that do well in any warm, sunny location; the fruit of several of the varieties grows quite large and is a desirable table delicacy.

Cœrulea. Large violet and blue flowers. 10 cents per pkt.
Incarnata. Whitish flowers with purple rays; edible fruits. 10 cents per pkt.
Von Volxemi (Tacsonia). Immense scarlet flowers. 15 cents per pkt.

PELARGONIUM.
(*Lady Washington Geranium*).

The seed of this new strain of "Perpetual Flowering Pelargoniums" has been specially saved for us from selected named specimens in the celebrated Sea Beach collection at Santa Cruz, California, and has been placed in our exclusive possession. The plants were over ten feet in height and covered with blooms of enormous size, while the colors and markings were unique and superb.

Perpetual Flowering. 25 cents per pkt.

NEMOPHILA.

Charming dwarf-growing annuals of compact habit and strikingly beautiful colors.

Insignis. Bright blue. 5 cents per pkt
Mixed. 5 cents per pkt.

Forty Flowering Bulbs for One Dollar ; see page 2 of Cover.

GROUP OF PHLOXES

PENSTEMON.

Beautiful hardy perennial, with flowers of various colors, produced on spikes.

Mixed. 5 cents per pkt.

PHLOX DRUMMONDII.

Well-known showy annuals, with brilliant and diversified colors, succeeding well everywhere; remains in bloom a long time.

Alba. Pure white. 5 cents per pkt.
Coccinea. Dazzling scarlet. 5 cents per pkt
Grandiflora. Large-flowered mixed. 10 cts. per pkt.
Isabellina. Pale yellow. 10 cents per pkt.
Nana Compacta. Dwarf varieties mixed. 10 cents per pkt.
Purpurea. Dark purple. 5 cents per pkt.
Rosea. Pale rose. 5 cents per pkt.
Mixed. Ordinary kinds. 5 cents per pkt

PETUNIA.

Valuable plants, succeeding almost anywhere; their rich colors and duration of bloom render them most desirable for garden or greenhouse decoration.

Crimson. Very rich color. 15 cents per pkt.
Double. The best mixture sold. 75 cents per pkt.
Grandiflora hybrida. Superb mixture. 25 cents per pkt.
Rose. Charming color. 25 cents per pkt.
Striped. Very beautiful. 15 cents per pkt.
White. Large pure, white flowers. 15 cents per pkt.

PINKS.

See *Dianthus.*

POPPY. (Papaver.)

Bright, easily grown annuals and perennials, embracing a wonderful range of charming colors, greatly admired by every one.

Carnation. Mixed bright colors. 5 cents per pkt.
Danebrog. Scarlet with white blotch. 10 cents per pkt.
Mikado. Double; laciniated petals, white, shading to pink and rose. 15 cents per pkt.
Pæony. Mixed. 5 cents per pkt.
Shirley. Of glossy, satiny texture; wide range of colors, sometimes edged with white. 10 cts. per pkt.
Umbrosum. Rich crimson with black blotch. 5 cents per pkt.
☞ One packet each of the above six annual varieties will be sent for 40 cents.

Nudicaule (Iceland Poppy). A beautiful class of bright, showy, dwarf perennials. 10 cents per pkt.
Orientale. Perennial, bright scarlet. 10 cents per pkt.

PORTULACA.

Brilliant, dwarf-growing annuals, luxuriating in warm situations, and blooming profusely the entire season.

Double. All colors mixed. 10 cents per pkt.
Single. Mixed. 5 cents per pkt.

PYRETHRUM AUREUM. (Golden Feather.)

Dwarf-growing bedding plant with bright yellow foliage; largely used and much admired for edging, etc.; the plants can be kept low, and the flower-spikes slipped out, showing a mass of yellow. 5 cts. per pkt.

Freesias flower in six months from seed. Try a packet.

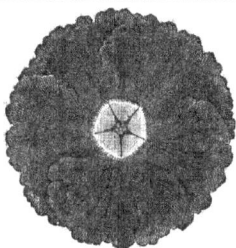

PRIMULA.

PRIMULA.

The Primrose is a universal favorite with all classes, the foliage being pretty and attractive, while the flowers furnish a wealth of charming colors.

Blue. Charming shade; beautifully fringed. 25 cents per pkt.
Crimson. Superb color, beautifully fringed. 25 cents per pkt.
Double. Splendid mixture. 75 cents per pkt
Fern-leaved. All colors mixed. 50 cents per pkt.
Pearl. Pure white, exquisitely fringed. 50 cents per pkt.
Rose. Very delicate; more fringed than others. 50 cents per pkt.
Scarlet. Bright, and beautifully fringed. 25 cents per pkt.
Superb Mixed. From the above. 25 cents per pkt.

RICINUS. (Castor-Oil Plant.)

Handsome, ornamental, rapid-growing foliage plants, with large, palm-like leaves, beautifully colored.

Borbonicusis arboreus. Immense foliage. 10 cents per pkt.
Gibsonii. Dark foliage, very attractive. 10 cents per pkt
Sanguineus. Red foliage. 5 cents per pkt.
Mixed. Many sorts, different from above. 5 cents per pkt.

SALPIGLOSSIS VARIABILIS GRANDIFLORA.

Highly ornamental annual, with large, veined, mottled, funnel-shaped flowers of many striking colors. Mixed. 10 cents per pkt.

SALVIA.

One of the handsomest flowering plants we have, being literally ablaze with brilliant flowers; very effective for massing on lawns or on the borders

Patens. Pure bright blue. 25 cents per pkt.
Splendens (Scarlet Sage). Intense scarlet. 10 cents per pkt.

RICINUS.

SENSITIVE PLANT. (Mimosa Pudica.)

An interesting and curious plant, with chaste and elegant foliage, the leaves being delicately pinnated. It affords much amusement, as when the leaves are slightly touched they instantly close and droop, as if about to die. 5 cents per pkt.

SENSITIVE PLANT.

SAPONARIA. CALABRICA.

A beautiful, dwarf, compact-growing plant, producing a mass of rich pink flowers, which continue in bloom the entire season. 5 cts per pkt.

STOCKS.

One of the most popular and beautiful favorites growing; brilliant and varied in color; no garden is complete without a few of these plants. The following are Large-flowered Dwarf Ten-weeks varieties:

Crimson. 15 cents per pkt
Rose. 15 cents per pkt.
White. 15 cents per pkt.
Yellow. 20 cents per pkt.
Mixed. All colors. 10 cents per pkt.

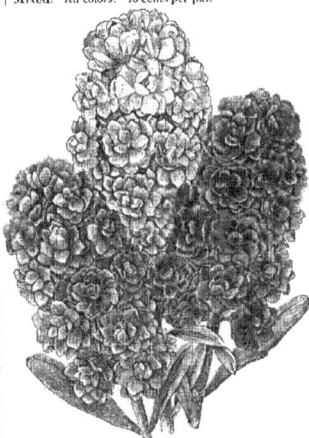

STOCK

Sweet Peas.

The "Hopkins Strain" of Sweet Peas, although of comparatively recent introduction, has gained an enviable reputation for superior quality, and wherever grown has called forth enthusiastic admiration. Until the advent of this marvellously improved strain, no such colors were dreamed of, and it is no exaggeration to state that in size and texture they far excel any other strain offered. The magnificent colored plate on the back cover has been drawn from nature, and conveys some idea of their exquisite beauty and large size.

Alba Magnifica. Pure white. 5 cents per pkt.
Apple Blossom. Bright rosy pink and blush. 5 cents per pkt.
Boreatton. Very dark crimson purple. 5 cts. per pkt.
Butterfly. White and lilac. 5 cents per pkt.
Captain of the Blues. Standards bright purple-blue, with pale blue wings; a very striking and fine variety. 10 cents per pkt.
Cardinal. Crimson scarlet. 5 cents per pkt.
Countess of Radnor. Pale mauve; magnificent. 15 cents per pkt.
Delight. Wings white; standards white, beautifully crested crimson; small but very pretty. 15 cents per pkt.
Dorothy Tennant. Dark mauve. 20 cents per pkt.
Duchess of Edinburgh. Scarlet and crimson. 5 cents per pkt.
Empress of India. Clear rosy pink standards; white wings; large and very pleasing. 15 cts. per pkt.
Fairy Queen. White and pink. 5 cents per pkt.
Her Majesty. Soft, rosy pink. 20 cents per pkt.
Ignea. Scarlet purple. 20 cents per pkt.
Isa Eckford. Creamy white and rosy pink. 5 cents per pkt.
Lemon Queen. Blush pink and lemon. 20 cents per pkt.
Miss Hunt. Carmine, salmon and soft pink. 10 cents per pkt.
Monarch. Bronze, crimson and blue. 20 cents per pkt.
Mrs. Eckford. Creamy white. 20 cents per pkt.

Mrs. Gladstone. Delicate pink standards; wings blush, edged with delicate pink; exquisite. 10 cents per pkt.
Mrs. Sankey. Pure white; a large, bold flower; fine improvement on whites; grand. 10 cents per pkt.
Nelly Jaynes. White and light pink. 5 cents per pkt.
Orange Prince. Orange pink. 5 cents per pkt.
Primrose. A near approach to yellow; quite novel and distinct in color; standards and wings pale primrose yellow. 15 cents per pkt.
Princess of Wales. Striped mauve on white ground. 5 cents per pkt.
Princess Victoria. Cherry, mauve, pink. 20 cents per pkt.
Purple Prince. Maroon standards, shaded with bronze and purple; blue wings; very fine and distinct. 10 cents per pkt.
Queen of England. White; of large size and good substance. 15 cents per pkt.
Red and White Striped. Choice. 5 cents per pkt.
Senator. Chocolate, creamy white. 20 cents per pkt.
Splendor. Pink rose, with crimson shading. 5 cents per pkt.
The Queen. Rosy pink and light mauve. 5 cents per pkt.
Waverley. Pale blue and rose. 20 cents per pkt.
ECKFORD'S NEW MIXED STRAIN, SPECIAL. Saved from choice unnamed varieties, including many of great merit. 10 cents per pkt.
Mixed. 5 cents per pkt.

Twenty-one of the best varieties Sweet Peas (see colored plate, back cover) sent for $1.50.

SMILAX.

Foliage and stems of a pleasing light green color, very graceful and delicate, and remain fresh for several days after being cut.

Myrsiphyllum Asparagoides. 5 cents per pkt.

SCABIOSA. (Mourning Bride.)

One of the most useful flowers for bouquets and decorative purposes; they make splendid clumps or masses by themselves or grouped with other flowers.

Mixed colors. 5 cents per pkt.

SEDUM CŒRULEUM. (Stonecrop.)

A dwarf plant, growing freely on rock-work, vases, old walls, etc. 10 cents per pkt.

SILENE. (Catchfly.)

Very showy, compact-growing, free-flowering plants, with bright and beautifully colored flowers.

Mixed colors. 5 cents per pkt.

SUNFLOWER. (Helianthus.)

This is an old and well-known flower; many of the new and best double varieties are attractive, and produce a fine effect among shrubbery or when used as screens.

Californicus fl. pl. Large and double. 5 cents per pkt.
Globosus Fistulosus. Immense double flowers. 5 cents per pkt.
Mammoth Russian. 5 cents per pkt.
Texas Silver Queen. Silky, silvery foliage. 10 cents per pkt.

SWEET WILLIAM.

The much improved forms in which this old and popular favorite is now offered render it more desirable than ever.

Mixed. Double and Single. 5 cents per pkt.

THUNBERGIA.

Slender, rapid-growing climbers, with extremely pretty and much admired flowers.

Mixed. All colors. 5 cents per pkt.

VERBENA.

A well-known and universal favorite, furnishing a c o n t i n u o u s bloom throughout the entire season.

Cœrulea. Beautiful blue. 5 cents per pkt.
Coccinea. Brilliant scarlet. 5 cents per pkt.
Lemon. The popular fragrant shrub. 5 cents per pkt.
Mammoth. Mixed colors of this recent introduction; flowers over twice the size of the old variety, 15 cents per pkt.
Striata. Beautifully striped. 5 cts. per pkt.
White. Of various shades. 5 cents per pkt.
Mixed. Ordinary variety. 5 cents per pkt.

VINCA.

Handsome, bushy plants, highly ornamental on account of their shining green foliage and handsome, circular flowers.

Alba. White, with crimson eye. 10 cents per pkt.
Rosea. Delicate pink. 10 cents per pkt.

VIOLET.

We grow Violets in very large quantities, and with great success. The seed we offer has been carefully saved from the best varieties grown at our nurseries at Menlo Park. For plants, see page 77.
Mixed. 10 cents per pkt.

VIRGINIAN STOCK.

Pretty profuse flowering little plants, remarkably effective in baskets or vases; grow freely anywhere.
Mixed. Red and white. 5 cents per pkt.

WALLFLOWER.

Greatly prized on account of their delicious fragrance, while their profuse blooming renders them exceedingly attractive.

Mixed. Double. 15 cents per pkt.
Mixed. Single. 5 cents per pkt.

ZEA JAPONICA.

A valuable ornamental foliage-plant, presenting a beautiful appearance, with broad foliage, striped white and green.

Fol. Variegata. 5 cents per pkt.

ZINNIA.

Annuals of great beauty and brilliancy, the effective display they make in the late season being simply unequalled.

Canary. Pale yellow. 5 cents per pkt.
Pompon. Small-flowered variety. 10 cents per pkt.
Rose. Salmon color. 5 cents per pkt.
Scarlet. Very brilliant. 5 cents per pkt.
Striped. 5 cents per pkt.
White. 5 cents per pkt.
Mixed. Large-flowered sorts. 5 cents per pkt.

VIOLETS.

Fertilizer, "Brand C," is a great Grass Invigorator.

PALM SEEDS.

	Pkt.	Per 100 seeds		Pkt.	Per 100 seeds
Areca Baueri (Norfolk Island Palm) . . . . 10 seeds, $0 25		$1 50	Kentia Belmoreana . . . . . . 10 seeds, $0 25		$2 00
" lutescens 10	" 25	1 50	" Forsteriana 10	" 25	2 00
" sapida 10	" 25	1 25	" Canterburyana 10	" 50	4 00
Caryota urens 10	" 25	2 00	" Morei 10	" 50	4 00
Chamaerops Canariensis . . . 10	" 25	1 25	Latania Borbonica 10	" 20	1 00
" excelsa 25	" 10	30	Musa Ensete 10	" 25	2 00
Cocos Weddeliana 8	" 25	2 50	Oreodoxa regia (Royal Palm) . 8	" 10	1 00
Corypha australis (Cabbage Palm) 10	" 10	60	Pandanus utilis (Screw Pine) . 10	" 25	1 50
Dracaena australis 20	" 10	25	Phœnix Canariensis 10	" 15	75
" indivisa 50	" 20	30	" dactylifera 10	" 10	75
Erythea armata 25	" 10	30	" reclinata 10	" 25	1 50
" edulis 25	" 10	30	" tenuis 8	" 10	1 00
			Ptychosperma Alexandræ . . 12	" 25	1 50
			Seaforthia elegans 8	" 10	1 00

"Wild Garden" Seeds.

Any one who has planted and cultivated flowers in neatly laid-out beds or carefully planned ribbon borders is aware of the amount of labor and constant attention necessary to produce a desirable effect. To those who cannot give this care, the "Wild Garden" presents a substitute which, for its unusual and varied effects, for economy, and the small amount of labor expended, has no rival. "Wild Garden" Seed is a mixture of over one hundred varieties of hardy flower seeds, and, being mixed together, can be offered at a much lower price than when sold in separate packets. One who has not seen such a bed is unable to form an idea of its possibilities, the successive seasons of bloom insuring something new well-nigh every day ; and the amount of beautiful flowers to be had in a season from such a bed is a great surprise. No attention need be given after sowing, but it is, of course, an advantage to enrich and thoroughly break up and make fine the ground before putting in the seed, in order that it may have an opportunity to germinate freely and bloom well.

Half-ounce packets, with full cultural directions, for 25 cents.

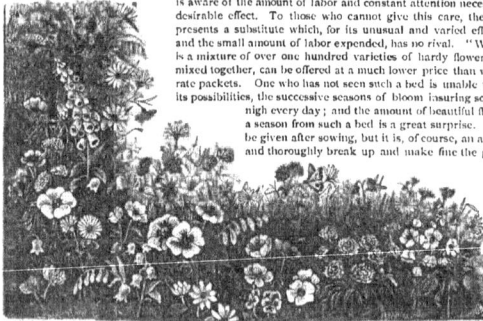

All packets in this Catalogue are 5 cents, except where noted.

Bulbous and other Flower=Roots.

*Varieties marked * cannot be supplied after November.*

	Each.	Doz.
AGAPANTHUS umbellatus (Blue African Lily). A graceful plant, producing large umbels of blue flowers	$0 35	
AMARYLLIS Belladonna major. Silvery white flowers, richly flushed with rosy red; very fragrant	40	
Formosissima (Jacobean Lily). Crimson-scarlet	25	
Johnsoni. Crimson, white-feathered	50	
Purpurea (*Vallota*). Brilliant scarlet	50	
ANEMONE fulgens (Scarlet Wind-Flower). Dazzling scarlet	$0 50	
Double Mixed . . . . per 100, $2		30
Single Mixed . . . . per 100, $2		30
BEGONIAS, Tuberous. Our collection of this beautiful flower is complete; the bulbs are of superior quality.		
Double Varieties. All colors mixed	40	4 00
Single Varieties. All colors mixed	20	2 00
BESSERA elegans. A splendid companion to *Milla biflora*; flowers scarlet, with a white band through the center of each petal		50

AMARYLLIS.

	Each Per doz.	
CALADIUM esculentum. A tropical plant growing to a height of four or five feet; immense leaves, often two feet broad. Extra-large bulbs,	$0 30	$3 00
Fancy-Leaved. Marvelous in variety of colors and markings	50	5 00
CALLA LILY (*Richardia Æthiopica*). Extra-sized bulbs,	25	2 50
Spotted (*Richardia alba marulata*). Foliage variegated with white; very handsome	30	3 00
Dwarf Calla Lily, "The Gem." This distinct novelty of more than ordinary merit seldom exceeds a height of ten inches, and produces from a bulb no larger than an ordinary Crocus three or four blooms of marvelous beauty. It is "The Gem" as a pot plant for window culture, and one that you cannot well afford to do without	40	4 00
***CROCUS, Blue, Purple, Striped, White and Yellow** . per 100, $1.50		25
All Colors Mixed . . . . per 100, $1		15

DWARF CALLA LILY, "THE GEM."

	Each.	Doz.
CALOCHORTUS. Known as Butterfly Tulip and Mariposa Lily. Produces cup-shaped flowers of the most charming and varied colors, peculiarly shaded, spotted, veined . per 100, $3		50
CYCLAMEN persicum giganteum. Extra-fine bulbs	25	2 50
DAHLIA, Double or Single. This favorite family of fall-flowering bulbs is too well known to require any description.		
Assorted Colors		$2 50
DIELYTRA or Bleeding-Heart. Flowers, borne on curved stalks, are delicate rose color and white, with purple lips, presenting when in full bloom a beautiful appearance	$0 35	
FREESIA refracta alba. Pure white and delightfully fragrant; largely used for forcing for cut flowers . . . . per 100, $2.00		50

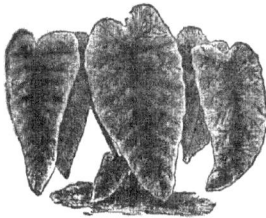

CALADIUM ESCULENTUM.

Special prices will be quoted for large quantities.

GLADIOLI.

Gladiolus.

These are the most easily grown and showy of all flowering bulbs, and are most effective when planted in clumps or beds. The wonderful beauty of our mixed sorts is beyond comparison, and wherever grown they are greatly admired. Our list of named sorts includes every good known variety.

	Each	Doz.
Africain. Staty brown on scarlet ground, streaked scarlet and pure white; white blotch	$0 25	$2 50
Angele. White; showy and effective . .	10	1 00
Brenchleyensis. Bright vermilion scarlet; a reliable sort for massing	5	50
Cleopatra. Flowers medium size, dark salmon, the lower petals profusely blotched purplish red, surrounded with straw color	15	1 50

	Each	Doz.
Ceres. White, spotted rose	$0 10	$1 00
Emma Thursby. White ground; carmine stripes through petals, blotch on the lower division	10	1 00
Enfant de Nancy. Flowers medium size, purplish red; lower petals dark crimson color, and blotching entirely unknown heretofore in Gladioli	15	1 50
Engesseri. Very deep pink; lower petals blotched bright maroon	15	1 50
Eugene Scribe. Tender rose, variegated	10	1 00
Freebell. Flesh colored, streaked with pink; carmine blotch, bordered with yellow	15	1 50
Gen. Phil. Sheridan. Fire-red, white lilac running running through each petal, and a large, pure white blotch on the lower division	20	2 00
Gen. Sherman. Large; fine scarlet . .	15	1 50
Incendiary. Flowers large; vermilion, rose colored throat; two lower petals scarlet-purple	15	1 50
Isaac Buchanan. Yellow	10	1 00
John Bull. White	10	1 00
La Candeur. White	15	1 50
Lafayette. Flowers very large, yellowish salmon; large crimson blotches on lower petals	15	1 50
Lamarck (de). Cherry	10	1 00
Lemoinei. Fine, good-sized flowers closely set on the spike, which is about one foot long; upper petals of a creamy white color, tinted salmon-red, the lower one spotted with deep purplish crimson, bordered with bright yellow and salmony red	15	1 50
Le Poussin. Light red, white blotch . .	10	1 00
Lord Byron. Brilliant scarlet, blotched pure white	10	1 00
Marie Dumortier. White, violet blotch	10	1 00
Marie Lemoine. Long spike of fine, well-expanded flowers; upper division of a pale creamy color, flushed salmon-lilac; lower divisions spotted purplish violet, bordered deep yellow	10	1 00
Martha Washington. Light yellow; of a large size, in a well-arranged spike; lower petals tinged with rose	10	1 00
Mme. Monneret. Delicate rose	10	1 00
Napoleon III. Scarlet, striped white . .	10	1 00
Obelisk. Flowers large, violet; lower petals blotched brown, spotted with sulphur	15	1 50
Princess of Wales. White, flamed carmine-rose	10	1 00
Shakespeare. White, suffused carmine-rose; large rosy blotch	15	1 50
Snow-White	25	2 50
Stella. White, slightly tinted with yellow and rose	10	1 00
Talma. Pale lilac, lower division violet-brown	10	1 00
W. E. Gumbleton. Flowers very large and open; purplish rose, streaked with rich carmine; spots velvet surrounded with yellow; plant unusually beautiful	15	1 50
ALL COLORS MIXED . per 100, $2 .	5	40
LIGHT COLORS MIXED. No red or dark colors. These are fine for bedding or masses . . . . per 100, $2.50 .	5	50

A trial will convince that "QUALITY" is our motto.

IXIAS.

	Each.	Doz.
HYACINTHS.* Finest mixed Double or Single, all colors	$1 00	$6 00
White Roman.* Very early	50	3 50
IRIS Kæmpferi. Beautiful Japanese variety. Single and Double, all colors mixed	25	2 50
IXIAS. For pot-culture in the house these never fail to please. The flowers resemble miniature Gladiolus, and are of most dazzling colors	25	1 50
JONQUILS.* Double and Single Sweet-scented	30	3 00

* Cannot be supplied after November.

Lilies.

The bulbs we offer are all home-grown, firm and fresh from the ground; not dried up and worthless, as is so often the case, and a frequent cause of failure. Bulbs should be allowed to remain undisturbed for years, frequent removals being injurious by destroying the roots.

	Each.	Per doz.
Auratum (Golden-Banded Lily of Japan). Pure white, studded with rich chocolate-crimson spots and a bright golden band through the center of each petal	$0 25	$2 50
Auratum Wittei. Pure white, with raised spots of satiny white; broad yellow stripe through each petal; immense flowers	1 00	10 00
Batemanniæ. Flowers of a bright apricot color	25	2 50
Brownii. Large flowers, white inside, purple outside; distinct and striking	1 00	10 00
Chalcedonicum. Scarlet; recurved blossoms	30	3 00
Coridion. Clear yellow; star-shaped flowers; exceedingly showy	20	2 00
Elegans Alice Wilson. A new variety, with upright yellow flowers	1 00	10 00
" atrosanguineum. Rich blood crimson	50	5 00
" flore semiplena. Magnificent flower; bright crimson, striped with pink; semi-double	75	7 50

	Each.	Doz.
Elegans Incomparable. Large, rich, blood-red flowers, spotted and splashed with lemon-yellow; very beautiful	$1 00	$10 00
Medeoloides. Orange-red with purple spots	50	5 00
Harrisii. (Bermuda Easter Lily.) Resembles *L. longiflorum*	20	2 00
Humboldtii. Reddish orange, spotted with purple	15	1 50
Krameri. Large, rose-colored flowers; fragrant	25	2 50
Longiflorum. Pure white, trumpet-shaped flowers	20	2 00

LILIUM AURATUM.

We will send ten varieties California Tree Seeds for One Dollar.

LILY-OF-THE-VALLEY.

LILIES, continued.

	Each.	Doz.
Parryii. Lemon yellow, spotted with brown	$0 30	$3 00
Speciosum album. Pure white, handsome flowers	30	3 00
roseum. White, shading to rose, spotted red	25	2 50
rubrum. Darker than the preceding	20	2 00
Tigrinum. (Common Tiger Lily) Orange with black spots	10	1 00
Washingtonianum. Changing from pure white to purple. Very fragrant	25	2 50

	Doz.	100.
LILY-OF-THE-VALLEY. Fragrant and beautiful pure white flowers; highly prized for bouquets. Strongflowering crowns	$0 40	$2 50
MILLA BIFLORA. Flowers are pure waxy white, star-shaped, and usually borne in pairs on long, slender stems	50	

MILLA BIFLORA.

	Doz.	100.
MONTBRETIA. In appearance resembles a miniature gladiolus, with bright orange-scarlet flowers with purple spots ; one of the most floriferous and showy little plants we have	$0 40	$2 50
NARCISSUS, Single and Double Mixed		50
Chinese Sacred Lily. Grown easily in water . . . . . . each, 15 cents		1 50
OXALIS. Colors separate		30
Mixed		25

TUBEROSE, "DWARF PEARL."

	Doz.	100.
RANUNCULUS. All colors mixed	$0 30	$2 00
SNOWDROPS. Single and double	30	2 00
TIGRIDIA (Mexican Shell Flower). Produces magnificent, showy flowers.		
Conchiflora. Yellow, spotted with crimson	50	3 00
Grandiflora. Crimson, with yellow center	50	3 00
alba. Pearl-white, with brown marking at base of the petals. A magnificent flower	1 00	7 50
TUBEROSES, Dwarf Pearl. The finest variety of this popular bulb	50	3 00
Tall Double	40	2 50
TULIPS,* Early Double. Mixed colors	40	2 50
Early Single. Mixed colors	40	2 50

Our Menlo Park Lawn Grass (see page 2) is Unsurpassed.

Nursery Department.

FOLIAGE AND FLOWERING PLANTS,
TREES, SHRUBS, VINES AND FRUIT TREES.

PACKING AND SHIPPING.—We have experienced packers to do the work, and all shrubs, trees, plants, vines, etc., will be thoroughly and securely packed, so that they can be safely shipped to any part of the country. We deliver to railroad and express companies free. There our responsibility ceases, and goods travel at purchaser's risk. That our customers should be fully satisfied with their purchase is our aim. Should they not be so, we wish to be informed of the fact without delay, so that we may be able to do justice to them and ourselves.

SUGGESTIONS TO PLANTERS.—The judicious and tasteful planting of trees and plants enhances the value of real estate more than an equal amount of money invested in any other way. The best time for planting is during the autumn and early spring. Success depends more upon the proper performance of the work, and on the weather during the following season, than on the exact time when the work is done. Trees, etc., should be planted somewhat deeper than they grew in the nursery; this is easily seen by the earth-stain on the bark. Do not twist or crowd the roots into a small space; dig a large hole, and carefully spread the roots out straight, fill the earth firmly around them and pack solid. Mulching with coarse manure, straw or leaves is beneficial to newly planted trees, and is the best means of retaining moisture in the soil. If the land is poor many trees do not grow luxuriantly for several years. Liberal watering should be given, but it is labor lost if imperfectly done; always soak the ground thoroughly when it needs it.

☞ **All Nursery Stock is quoted free to express or railroad at our Nurseries at Menlo Park, Cal.**

Orchids.

We offer a few selected Orchids, which will be found to do well under ordinary treatment. They are all beautiful varieties.

CYPRIPEDIUM (Lady's Slipper). These are very easily cultivated. A soil of peat and moss, with ample drainage, in clean pots, selecting a moist and rather shady corner of the greenhouse, will suit them admirably.

C. Boxalli. This variety flowers from December to January; is very attractive; flowers have a very bright and shiny appearance. $2.50 each.

C. Dominianum. Flowers in the autumn; three to five on long stems. $2.75 each.

C. Harrisianum. Flowering twice, and sometimes three times, in the course of a year. $2.50 each.

C. insigne. This variety lasts in flower over a long period, and will be found very satisfactory. $1 ea.

C. villosum. Flowers from January to April. $2.50 each.

CATTLEYA. In growing this Orchid use fibrous peat and a little moss. In potting, keep the plant well above the rim of the pot, and leave the soil so that the water will pass away freely, plenty of which must be used during the growing season. After new bulbs are developed, water should be withheld and the plant allowed a good season of rest.

C. Trianæ. One of the most beautiful Orchids in cultivation; flowering from December to April; colors varying from pure white to blush; the throat yellow, with a bright crimson spot on the lip. $3 each.

C. Percivaliana. Very choice; flowers from November to February. $3 each.

C. Mossiæ. Large, sweet scented flowers; colors lilac and rose. $3 each.

CŒLOGYNE cristata. A fine winter flowering Orchid, very easily grown; flower white, with yellow blotch on the lip. January to March. $1.50 each.

DENDROBIUM nobile. This Orchid flowers on the long pseudo-bulbs in twos and threes; colors white and the various shades of purple. $1.50 each.

LÆLIA Anceps. A very beautiful species, flowering about Christmas, when it is all the more welcome; flowers purple and blush, on long and graceful stems. $1.50 each.

ODONTOGLOSSUM crispum. Flowers mostly from January to April; should be kept cool and moist, never being allowed to get dry; very attractive. All the Odontoglossums are showy and valuable for cutting. $1.50 each.

CYPRIPEDIUM INSIGNE.

Our Stock of "Selected Seeds" is all new and very high in quality.

Decorative Plants.

These plants are generally grown in the greenhouse, and used for the decoration of windows, hallways, etc. We carry a very fine collection, a few of which are listed below.

PANDANUS.

ACALYPHA marginata. A very ornamental nettle-like leaved greenhouse shrub.

ARALIA filicifolius. A valuable plant, with finely divided foliage of singular beauty and distinctiveness; stem and leaf stalks are purplish, with white spots; very effective. $2 each.

ASPIDISTRA lurida. Hardy, or nearly hardy, evergreen foliage plants. 75 cents each.

A. lurida var. This variety has a white band running through some of the leaves. 75 cents each.

BEGONIAS. We have a fine strain of single and double tuberous-rooted Begonias; plants well established in pots, 50 cents each and $1 each.

CROTON interruptum. A bright-foliaged decorative plant for the greenhouse. $1.50 each.

CURCULIGO recurvata. A very ornamental greenhouse plant of palm-like growth and easy culture. $1 each.

DIEFFENBACHIA picta. Leaves bright green, spotted with white. $1 each.

EUCHARIS Amazonica. Known as the Amazon Lily. Strong, flowering bulbs in pots, 25 cts. each.

ASPIDISTRA LURIDA VARIEGATA.

DRACÆNA. Valuable greenhouse and outdoor decorative plant, some varieties being variously banded with white and brown and pink stripes

D. Braziliensis. Robust-growing, with large, broad, green foliage. $1 each.

D. Guilfoylei. Bright green, striped with white and red. $1.50 each.

D. Lindeni. Foliage bright green, banded with creamy white. $2 each.

D. Mooreana. Crimson, changing to glossy bronze. $1 each.

D. nigricans. Very dark foliage; distinct. $1 ea.

D. spectabilis. Foliage long, green; very graceful. $1.50 each.

D. indivisa. Similar to *D. australis*, but more erect in growth; good both for outdoor and greenhouse work. Plants 2 feet high, $1.50; smaller plants, 75 cents each.

D. australis. A very useful variety for planting on lawns and avenues. Plants 5 and 6 feet high, $6 ea.

DRACÆNA INDIVISA

PILE Amicrophylla. The Aartillery or Pistol plant $1 each

PANDANUS. Valuable decorative plants, commonly called the Screw Pine.

P. Veitchii. A very useful house plant, with long, variegated leaves. $1.50 each.

P. Caricosus. A variety of dwarf habit; long, green foliage. $1 each.

POINSETTIA. This well-known plant, so much used in decoration at Christmas, should be in every greenhouse. Plants in 6-inch pots, 75 cents each

RHODEA Japonica variegata. A most beautiful decorative plant, somewhat resembling *Aspidistra lurida var.* $1 each.

SANCHEZIA nobilis. Leaves of green color, striped with white. $1 each.

Our Collections of Seeds, Plants and Bulbs are of great value.

Ferns, Etc.

These most beautiful plants are grow'ng constantly in favor for decoration and for cutting We offer only the best and most distinct sorts.

ADIANTUM Farleyense. One of the grandest varieties of Adiantum ; requires warm greenhouse treatment, and should never be allowed to get dry. No collection is complete without this variety. 53 to $5 each.

A. cuneatum (Maiden Hair). One of the best known Adiantums ; generally used with cut-flowers. 75 cts. to $2 each.

ASPLENIUMS. A very pretty genus of Ferns ; suitable for pots or baskets. 75 cts. each.

ASPARAGUS plumosus. A beautiful evergreen climber, with spreading branches ; it forms an excellent pot plant, and is also very desirable for cutting. $1.50 each.

A. plumosus nanus. An improved variety of the above. $2 and $3 each.

A. tenuissimus. A tall-growing variety with very graceful branchlets ; much used in decorative work. 35 and 50 cents each ; large plants, $1.

CYPERUS alternifolius. An elegant greenhouse plant of compact habit, with long, narrow green leaves arrayed in an umbellate manner at the end of the stems—hence its name, Umbrella plant. 50 cents and $1 each.

PTERIS Cretica albo-lineata. Very desirable for table and other decorations. 50 cts. and $1 each.

PALM, PHŒNIX CANARIENSIS.

Palms.

For decorative purposes, Palms are very valuable, and in late years their popularity has grown in a remarkable manner. We offer a select assortment of the best only.

ARECA lutescens. One of the best Palms for decorative purposes. $1.50 each.

CHAMÆROPS excelsa. A very hardy Palm, with dark green, fan-shaped leaves. Plants from field, 75 cts. each ; large plants in boxes, $5 each.

KENTIA Belmoreana and K. Forsteriana. Two very useful Palms for house decoration. $1.50 each.

LATANIA borbonica. The leaves of this variety are very much reflexed, making it a very handsome specimen plant ; especially suitable for table decoration. Sold in immense quantities in the east$. 1 50 each.

PHŒNIX Canariensis. The hardiest and most beautiful of the Date Palm family ; very desirable for planting on lawns and avenues. $1 each.

PRITCHARDIA filifera. The well-known Fan Palm ; of erect, rapid growth, with immense fan-shaped leaves of a light green color, with hair-like filaments attached. Our stock of this variety is especially fine. Plants from the field, two feet high, 75 cents and $1 each, $65 per 100, $500 per 1,000.

SEAFORTHIA elegans. Leaves pinnate, of a dark green, the divisions being very narrow ; an elegant and useful variety. $1 each.

S. Alexandria. Similar to above ; of a lighter green color. $1 each.

LATANIA BORBONICA.

We carry a full stock of Fern and Palm Seeds.

LA FRANCE.

· ROSES.

We offer a select list of Roses covering all the really desirable sorts grown, but excluding mere duplications which afford no real distinct features. Our California climate is superb for Roses, and we know our friends will be glad for the fine assortment here presented.

We divide the sorts for convenience into several classes: The HYBRID PERPETUALS, including also the Moss and Banksia Roses; the TEA or EVERBLOOMING Roses, including Hybrid Teas, Climbing Teas, China, Bourbon and Bengal, divisions and the new Polyantha Roses.

☞ **OUR SPECIAL OFFER:** To avoid the disappointments which unsatisfactory selections often entail, we make the following very *low offer*, in the hope that our customers will leave the selection of varieties to us. None but reliable kinds shall be sent, which will give better satisfaction, often, than the purchaser's selection.

	10	100
DWARF HYBRID PERPETUALS	$2 00	$17 50
STANDARD HYBRID PERPETUALS	8 50	75 00
TEA or EVERBLOOMING	2 00	17 50

☞ *Where the price of Standards is omitted, we can only supply the variety as Dwarfs.*

Hybrid Perpetual Roses.

These are the hardy Roses of the east, and are brilliant in coloring and stately in form. They range from pure white through lovely flesh and pink shades to deep, blackish crimson, but include no positive shades of yellow. The Moss and Banksia classes, included here for convenience, are both desirable.

25 cents each for dwarfs, unless otherwise noted.

A. K. Williams. Bright crimson; good form.

Aimee Vibert. (Moss.) Pure white.

Alfred Colomb. Bright fiery red; one of the finest Roses in cultivation.

Ampere. Rich purplish red, tinged with lilac

Anna Alexieff. Rose color; large, full flowers, freely produced. Standards, $1 each.

Anna de Diesbach. The most lovely shade of carmine.

Antoine Mouton. Fine, bright rose; almost as large as Paul Neyron.

Auguste Mie. Clear, bright pink.

Banksia White. Pure, clear white; very double.

Baron de Bonstetten. Very dark red, almost black. Standards, $1 each

Baron N. de Rothschild. Flowers large, full and double; bright carmine.

Baroness Rothschild. Bright pink; large, handsome flower. Standards, $1 each.

Capt. John Ingraham. (Moss.) Dark, velvety purple.

Chas. Lefebvre. Velvety crimson; large.

Cheshunt Hybrid. Red, shaded with violet; huge, full. Standards, $1 each

---

If you receive two Catalogues, give your neighbor one.

PURITAN.

Comtesse H. de Choiseul. Flesh color; salmon-pink center.
Duchess of Bedford. Fiery crimson; large, full and perfect.
Duke of Connaught. Rosy crimson; large, full, good in bud.

Duke of Edinburgh. Fine vermilion; large, full, of good shape. Standards, $1 each.
Earl Dufferin. Rich, velvety crimson; very large; splendid form.
Empress of India. Dark brownish crimson; large and full. Standards, $1 each
Fisher Holmes. Magnificent scarlet, imbricated; large and full.
Francois Level. Cherry rose, medium size.
Geant des Battailles. Brilliant fiery crimson.
Gen. Jacqueminot. Brilliant scarlet crimson; large and magnificent
Glory of Mosses. (Moss.) Pink; very pretty.
Her Majesty. The largest rose in cultivation; delicate, but bright pink.
James Veitch. Deep violet, shaded crimson.
John Hopper. Deep pink; large, full; good bloomer.
Louis Van Houtte. Velvety crimson, very large and full; a grand rose.
Mabel Morrison. A white form of Baroness Rothschild
Madame Chas. Wood. Crimson, shaded purple.
Madame Gabriel Luziet. Beautiful satiny pink; very large.
Magna Charta. Fine, bright pink; very large, double and fine form.
Marchioness of Lorne. Rich red, shaded in center with carmine.
Marshall P. Wilder. Carmine; an excellent variety
Mrs. J. Laing. Clear pink; very fragrant; a splendid variety.
Paul Neyron. Deep pink; very large and full; largest in cultivation.
Princess of Wales. Outside petals rosy yellow; center rich, golden yellow.
Puritan. Flowers white, large, pure and sweet. Standards, $1 each.
Sweet Briar. Sweetly perfumed.
White Bath. (Moss.) White, sometimes tinged with pink.
White Baroness. White; similar to Mabel Morrison

Tea or Everblooming Roses.

A most popular class, because of their habit of constant bloom while growing, and because of their lovely buds. The range of color is very wide, and includes beautiful yellow shades. Nearly all are fragrant and of rather bushy habit; some are climbers. The Hybrid Teas are here included also; these combine the qualities of both classes, as evidenced in La France, the best of the kind, and a superb Rose. The Polyanthas are very dwarf and floriferous, and serve well to edge beds of other Roses.

Aline Sisley. Color varying from red to purplish rose.
American Beauty. Deep pink, very large; good for forcing.
Agrippina. Rich, velvety crimson.
Bon Silene. Noted for the size and beauty of the buds; deep rose color.
Capt. Christy. Delicate flesh color, deeper in center. Standards, $1 each.
Celine Forester. Pale yellow, deeper towards center. Standards, $1 each.
Catherine Mermet. A beautiful rose; color clear shining pink. Standards, $1 each.
Cloth of Gold. Deep yellow center, with sulphur edges. Standards, $1 each.
Coquette de Lyon. Canary yellow; medium size, fine form. Standards, $1 each.
Cornelia Cook. Large, fine buds; creamy white. Standards, $1 each.
Duchess of Albany. Shape of La France; deeper in color. Standards, $1 each.
Duchess de Brabant. Soft, silvery flesh, changing to deep rose. Standards, $1 each.
Duchess of Connaught. Crimson, shaded with brownish tint. Standards, $1 each.
Duchess of Edinburgh. Flowers of good substance.
Devoniensis. Beautiful creamy white and rosy center.

GEANT DES BATTAILLES.

What do you think of the last page of the cover?

![PERLE DES JARDINS.]

PERLE DES JARDINS.

Dr. Grill. Coppery yellow; very pretty. Standards, $1 each.

Eliza Savage. Yellow to white; a profuse bloomer. Standards, $1 each.

Etoile de Lyon. Beautiful chrome yellow; center golden yellow.

Gloire de Dijon. Buff orange center; fine climber.

Hermosa. Bright rose; a most constant bloomer.

Jean Sisley. Flowers large; color outside petals rosy lilac, center bright pink.

Letty Coles. Soft, rosy pink.

La Marque. Pure white; good bloomer.

La France. Bright lilac-pink; center silvery white. (See cut, page 56.)

Madame de Watteville. Color a shade of creamy yellow, richly tinged with carmine.

Marechal Niel. Bright, golden yellow; unquestionably the best rose grown.

Marie Guillot. White, faintly tinged with yellow.

Meteor. Rich, velvety crimson; free flowering.

Madam Cecil Brunner. (Polyantha.) Clear, rosy pink, double and sweet; very floriferous.

Niphetos. Pure white; one of the best bloomers.

Papa Gontier. Extra large, fine formed buds and flowers; color brilliant carmine.

Perle des Blanches. One of the finest whites.

Perle des Jardins. Straw color; buds of perfect form; one of the very best.

Reine Marie Henriette. Large, compact, fully formed flowers; color cherry red

Safrano. Salmon-buff; good; one of the best bloomers. Standards, $1 each.

Shirley Hibberd. Beautiful, nankeen-yellow; small flowers. Standards, $1 each.

Souv. d'un Ami. Salmon rose; large and very fine.

Souv. de la Malmaison. Clear flesh; large and double; has been a general favorite for more than a generation. Standards, $1 each.

Souv. de Wootton. Bright red; good forcer.

Sunset. Rich orange or saffron; sport from Perle des Jardins. Standards, $1 each.

The Queen. White; profuse bloomer, a most beautiful rose. Standards, $1.25 each.

The Bride. An everblooming Tea rose, of large size and most perfect form. Standards, $1 each.

Waban. Sport from Catherine Mermet, but of a brighter color; one of the best of the newer roses.

W. A. Richardson. Beautiful, orange-yellow; well formed.

W. F. Bennett. Extra fine buds of the most brilliant crimson.

25 cents each for dwarfs, unless otherwise noted.

Our goods speak for themselves; everybody says so.

CARNATIONS.

Field-grown, good stock, 25 cents each, $20 per 100 ; pot-grown, good stock, 15 cents each, $12.50 per 100.

American Flag. White, striped with scarlet.

Annie Wiegand. Clear, delicate pink ; long, stout stems ; an early and free bloomer.

Attraction. Extremely showy ; bright, rosy scarlet ; nicely fringed and double ; good stems and perfect calyx. A color universally admired.

Ben Hur. Soft pink, of the Wilder shade, but brighter ; petals broad and heavy ; stems long and stout ; an exquisite variety and fine grower.

Cherry Lips. As its name implies, this is a beautiful cherry-red ; very desirable.

Creole. Velvety maroon, occasionally flaked with carmine ; strong stems

Dark Scarlet. A rich shade, and very free flowering.

Daybreak. Clear, bright flesh without shading ; large ; long flower stems.

Fred. Creighton. Delicate shade of pink, similar to Grace Wilder.

Fred. Dorner. Clear, deep scarlet ; large and double, fringed.

Grace Wilder. Soft shade of rosy pink ; one of the most beautiful

Hinze's White. Pure white, large flowers ; free bloomer ; one of the best.

J. R. Freeman. A rare shade of rich carmine ; early and free ; fragrant ; long stems

La Purite. A very desirable shade of carmine ; well formed flowers.

Lizzie McGowan. Pure white ; very large, full and heavy ; compact grower ; cut-flowers keep well

Lu-Lu. Pretty shade of pink ; fine for growing in pots.

Mrs. Hitt. Free-growing and very long-stemmed ; flower large and of fine form ; calyx perfect ; glowing pink.

Nelly Bly. Salmon pink, striped and splashed with red.

Portia. Intense flaming scarlet ; vigorous grower ; flowers freely produced on long stems. $15 per 100

Puritan. White ; large, very full and of good substance, lasting, if well-grown, a long time after being cut ; quite fragrant and an early and continuous bloomer.

Silver Spray. Pure white ; stiff, upright stems ; early and free.

Springfield. An exquisite shade of pink ; very pretty and sweet.

Thos. Cartledge. Carmine, closely resembling La Purite in color ; vigorous grower ; early and prolific

Tidal Wave. Dark red ; dwarf.

White Dove. A grand pure white fringed variety of large size ; stems quite stiff and very long, foliage heavy.

White Wings. Purest white ; petals heavy, silvery surface ; large, lightly fringed ; profuse bloomer.

Chrysanthemums.

Our people of the Golden Coast know what beauty there is for them in the Chrysanthemum, the autumn Queen of the East, and are taking great interest in this superb flower. We provide in the following list a rare collection of the very best varieties grown; none better can be had anywhere or at any price. Our display of Chrysanthemums at Menlo Park is gorgeous to look upon.

New Varieties.

Miss Annie Manda. Flowers very high and compact, perfectly double, incurved, of the purest white; the numerous petals are well furnished with long, glandular, hair-like outgrowth, giving the flower a unique appearance, far surpassing the celebrated Mrs. Alpheus Hardy; the plant is of strong and vigorous habit, carrying the flower erect on a stout stem; another recommendation is that the flower is sweetly scented.

W. A. Manda. The New Golden Yellow Hairy Chrysanthemum. Flower very large, of a clear golden yellow color; the plant is vigorous in growth, and the flower is borne upright on a stout stem; this is the grandest introduction from Japan made during the past year, and no collection can afford to be without this variety.

Mr. H. Ballantine. Flower rather flat, showing the center somewhat; of a beautiful old-gold or bronzy color; a free grower and a good acquisition.

Marble. Flower pure white, of medium size; the strongly incurving petals evenly imbricated, giving the flower a compact and solid appearance.

Pearl Shell. Flower very large, semi-double, of a beautiful pale pink; a free-growing plant.

Nacre. Flower large, almost double, of a fine silvery pink color; petals incurved.

Alabaster. Flower large, white, with a yellow center, borne upright on a stout stem; petals incurving.

Chastity. Large, full flower; white, with a yellow center; petals strongly incurved.

Simplicity. Flower of good size; white, with green center; petals incurved.

Vanity. Flower large, semi-double, of a lilac-pink color; petals sparingly hairy and incurved.

Purity. Flower very large, single; pure white, with a large, yellow, button-like center; petals very broad, slightly reflexing.

Roslyn. A superb, clear, Mermet rose-pink; petals thick and heavy, cup-shaped, solid to the center; immense in size, having been exhibited eleven inches across; habit the best; stems stiff and erect; foliage luxuriant; the best pink in commerce. Awarded Silver Medal, Pennsylvania Horticultural Society; Certificate of Merit, Madison Square Garden, New York, and was one of the sorts winning the Spaulding prize at Philadelphia for best six new seedlings.

Dr. Covert. A magnificent, incurving, deep golden yellow, of great substance; very bright and attractive; perfectly double, carried on stiff stems; an excellent grower; a grand variety to follow Widener in season of blooming.

Edward Hatch. One of the grandest offerings of the year. An immense incurving variety; depth about equal to its diameter; color soft lemon and bright pink. Awarded silver cup at Madison Square for best pink seedling; also, first-class certificate New York and Indianapolis.

Fred. Dorner. Opens with incurving center and recurving outer petals, gradually resolves into a large pyramid of recurving petals; very pleasing creamy white, with light lines of palest pink. First premium as finest seedling at the last Orange, N. J., show.

Jno. Bertermann. A very large flower of heavy texture and regular, recurving form; color creamy white; a fine grower; flowers borne on stiff stems.

Joseph H. White. A splendid white variety, with upright petals forming a half globe; very double; of heavy substance; in every way a grand white. First-class certificate at both New York and Boston.

Shenandoah. Magnificent, broad flower, full and double to the center, over an inch in width; color a new shade of deep chestnut-brown on both upper and lower surface, the entire flower being a solid color without shadings; novel and distinct. Prize winner at Philadelphia.

E. Hitzeroth. A magnificent, extra-large flower; petals broad and peculiarly arranged, completely filling the center; bright lemon-yellow; novel form; fine for commercial or exhibition purposes. Awarded the Winslow cup at Madison Square Garden, New York, for best yellow; also Certificate of Merit.

Lillian Russell. A beautiful, broad-petaled variety; clear silvery pink; incurved, forming an immense round ball of largest size; an early flowering sort, suitable for all purposes. Was among the collection winning the Astor Cup at Madison Square Garden.

Marguerite Jeffords. An immense ball of bright amber; very full, and grows as a perfect incurving specimen plant. Secured the Whilldin prize at the Philadelphia show.

CHRYSANTHEMUM FIELD AT MENLO PARK NURSERIES.

We guarantee satisfaction, because we know what we sell.

NEW CHRYSANTHEMUMS, continued.

Peerless. Flower of loose texture; white, with yellow center; a good grower.

Ada H. Le Roy. Symmetrically formed; petals broad and cupped full to the center; color deep rose-pink; extra-large flower; one of the best for exhibition purposes. Certificate of merit by Pennsylvania Horticultural Society.

Col. Wm. B. Smith. An immense, double, high-built flower; petals broad and large, forming a solid mass of the richest bright golden bronze. Awarded at Madison Square Garden Exhibition Certificate of Merit, also the Bird Cup for best seedling not yet in commerce; Certificate of Merit by Pennsylvania Horticultural Society.

Ruth Cleveland. A chaste and beautiful acquisition; large size; petals broad, cup-shaped, outer petals reflexed, inner ones incurved, forming a high-built center of most delicate silvery pink. This variety having been registered, is the only one recognized by the American Chrysanthemum Society under this name. One of the collection winning the Astor Cup.

H. F. Spaulding. A grand Japanese variety of novel shape and effect; color rich apricot-yellow, shading to rose, center petals clear yellow; bloom solid and double; high-built and of largest size; similar in shape to a pineapple; habit strong and robust. Awarded the Ladenburg Cup at Madison Square Garden Exhibition, also Certificate of Merit.

J. N. May. Extra-large; deep ox-blood red, color of Mrs. J. T. Emlin, but much larger and more double; reverse of petals shaded coppery bronze; full, solid flower; fine.

Mrs. J. W. Morrissey. A mammoth flower, with full, double center—exhibited twelve inches across; color silvery pink, inner surface of petals bright rose; a grand exhibition bloom. Awarded Certificate of Merit by Pennsylvania Horticultural Society.

Eva Hoyte. An immense, double, Japanese bloom of clearest and brightest yellow; a solid ball, with full, high-built center; grand for any purpose, and superior to Widener and other existing varieties for exhibition purposes. Two hundred and fifty dollars was paid for the control of this magnificent yellow.

A. Ladenburg. A full and extremely double Japanese variety; immense size, having been grown ten inches across; style and shape of Mrs. I. Clark, except in color, which is a clear, delicate rose-pink; magnificent for exhibition purposes. Awarded Certificate of Merit by Pennsylvania Horticultural Society, also at Madison Square Garden Exhibition.

Mrs. Robert Craig. A snow-white variety; has the perfect incurving form of the best Chinese, together with the grandeur in size and heavy texture of the Japanese; of unsurpassed beauty. Silver Medal at Philadelphia, Certificate at Madison Square, N. Y., and Indianapolis.

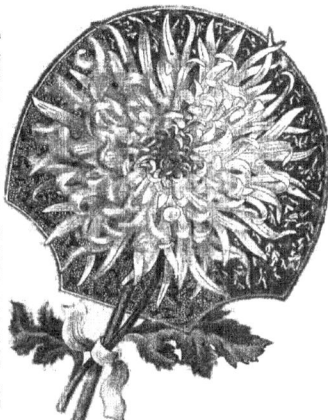

JAPANESE CHRYSANTHEMUM.

Mrs. Maria Simpson. Broad, heavy petals, gracefully incurving; a perfect Japanese variety; color rich chrome-yellow; one of the largest in size. Silver Medal at Philadelphia, Certificate at Indianapolis.

Mrs. L. C. Madeira. Probably the finest specimen extant in the Chinese section; it forms a large, compact, bright orange ball; very heavy petals, like an unopened, slightly incurving, quilled variety, nicely pointed; destined to become a leader, being a distinct advance in its section. Silver Medal at Philadelphia, Certificate at Indianapolis.

Mrs. A. J. Drexel. An early variety; color rich, velvety crimson-maroon; very large for its season; will be much appreciated by those seeking large, early-flowering sorts of rich color. Certificate at New York.

O. P. Bassett. The finest crimson-scarlet ever introduced; a giant Cullingfordii—identical in color when Cullingfordii is at its best, and as large as Canning; very velvety, and will undoubtedly prove a great acquisition. First premium at Indianapolis, and Certificate at both New York and Philadelphia.

Price, 50 cents each, $5 per dozen. Ready to ship March 1st.

Prize Single-Flowered Chrysanthemums.

Newark. Large, pure white flower, with very broad and thick, round petals.

Newton. A fine, free grower, with large flowers of rose-pink color.

Trenton. Large, pure white flower, with narrow, pointed petals.

Princeton. Large flower of bright golden yellow, with pointed petals.

Camden. Large, lilac-pink flower, with tubular, spatulate petals.

Salem. Flower of salmon-rose, with tubular spatulate petals.

Boonton. Large, rose-pink flowers, with narrow, pointed petals.

Rahway. Large, white flower, with reflexed, pointed petals.

Hackensack. Very large flower of lovely pale pink; petals strongly spoon-shaped.

Mitford. Flower pure white, with long, narrow petals.

Orange. Flower bright golden yellow, with large, broad petals.

Burlington. Flower pure white, with long, tubular petals.

20 cents each, $2 per dozen.

"QUALITY" is our watchword, and our Prices are Reasonable.

JAPANESE CHRYSANTHEMUM.

Prize Reflexed Chrysanthemums.

Mrs. E. D. Adams. Flower very large; petals of medium width, very long, twisted, the outer ones swirled, as if the flower had been turned swiftly on its stem; color pure white; one of the best and most distinct white Chrysanthemums in cultivation; we have specimens measuring thirteen inches over the flower from tip to tip of petals; makes a grand bush plant, and always attracts great attention when shown.

Mrs. W. S. Kimball. Flower very large, full, double; pale blush or creamy white, with a yellowish center; petals very broad, reflexed; one of the finest varieties for exhibition purposes.

Miss Ada McVicker. A plant of strong habit, producing immense, creamy white flowers, with broad, thick, reflexed petals; a grand variety, and one of the best for either specimen blooms, bush plants or standards.

Mrs. J. Hood Wright. Flower large, full double, of the purest white, with reflex, twisted petals; a strong grower, and one of the finest early varieties in cultivation.

Col. H. M. Boles. A plant of vigorous habit, producing very large, rose-pink flowers with twisted petals, veined with a lighter shade; very full center; a grand exhibition variety.

Frances Tarbox. Large flower, with full center petals broad, convexed, silvery pink, with a narrow line of pale lilac at the extreme edge; a fine early-flowering variety.

Mrs. Herbert Leon. Flower very large, full double pink, with broad, reflexed petals; a very fine early variety.

Mrs. Gallagher. Flower large, semi-globular, with full center; petals deep maroon-crimson above, paler below; one of the very best dark varieties.

Mrs. E. D. Church. One of the earliest varieties in cultivation; flower full double, of medium size, borne on stout stems, and lasting long in perfection; color pink, in various shades.

Mrs. R. Benner. Flower medium size, of a deep lilac-pink color, with a red center; a very striking late variety.

Baby Cleveland. Flower semi-globular, full, double, of medium size, with broad petals; color lilac-pink— a very fine and telling color among Chrysanthemums.

Mr. A. G. Ramsey. Flower of medium size, full center; petals broad, upper surface of the expanded limb deep Indian-red, yellowish at the tip; under surface yellowish, veined with lines of red; a striking sort.

20 cents each, $2 per dozen. Ready to ship March 1st.

Our Menlo Park Lawn Grass (see page 2) is unsurpassed.

Prize Incurved Chrysanthemums.

Harry May. Flower very large and deep, full double, forming, when well opened, a massive sphere ; color deep old gold, with occasional veins of red : petals very broad and thick, spoon-shaped ; foliage very luxuriant, thick and leathery, deep green, and quite distinct among Chrysanthemums ; one of the most vigorous growing of all varieties in cultivation, and unsurpassed for growing either as a standard, as a bush plant, or for cut blooms for exhibition purposes.

Miss M. Colgate. Flower perfectly hemispherical, compact with a full center ; pure white ; petals broad, incurved ; a grand, pure white variety ; a strong grower and free-flowerer ; good for all exhibition purposes.

Mr. Hicks Arnold. A strong-growing and floriferous variety, bearing large, full double flowers of an old-gold color, lighting up wonderfully by artificial light ; when fully open the flower is almost spherical ; the freest growing variety known, and one which may be grown with success for almost any purpose.

Mrs. Dr. H. A. Mandeville. Large flower, perfectly spherical, with broad, incurved petals of a terra-cotta-yellow ; plant of vigorous habit and good for exhibition purposes.

Miss Bertha N. Robison. Flower rose-pink with red center ; very early, of large size and good substance ; one of the earliest and best varieties for exhibition purposes, either as pot plants or cut flowers.

Mr. D. S. Brown. Flower medium size, semi-double, of a clear, canary-yellow color when first opening, but changes to cream color as the petals expand ; a distinct color.

George Savage. Flowers very large, pure white, with broad, strongly incurved petals, making the flower almost hemispherical and very solid ; a grand variety of vigorous, free-growing habit, and useful for cut blooms for exhibition.

Mrs. John Eyerman. Flower semi-globular, full double petals, decidedly spoon-shaped, the lower half being tubular, while the limb is broadly expanded ; upper surface rose-pink, lower pale lilac ; a grand variety for exhibition purposes.

Dr. H. A. Mandeville. Flower large, full double, bright chrome-yellow ; petals very long and twisted, with a swirled habit, the upper incurved, while the lower are reflexed towards the stem ; one of the grandest varieties in cultivation.

Mohican. Flower large, of a deep mahogany color ; petals incurved, covering the center well when fully expanded ; plant of vigorous growth and habit, and the flower of a distinct color in collections.

Pawnee. Flowers very large ; Indian-red, with yellow shadings ; massive, incurved ; a fine, late-flowering variety.

Mrs. T. F. Mercer. Flower large, blush white ; petals broad, incurved, the inner regularly imbricated, the outer more spreading ; one of the best varieties for exhibition purposes, and valuable on account of its late flowering.

**20 cts. each, $2 per doz.
Ready to ship Mar. 1.**

INCURVED CHRYSANTHEMUM.

Anemone-Flowered Varieties.

This is a remarkable class, the flowers being almost fantastic in shape. They show a high, cushion-like center, with splendid petals surrounding it.

Herald. One of the grandest of the section ; flowers very large, bright golden yellow ; the center florets tubular, large, an inch or more long, notched at the rim, and crowded into a compact head ; ray petals in a single row, very long, drooping with age.

Egret. Flower of medium size ; pure white ; central petals strap-shaped, standing upright ; ray petal in a single row, reflexed.

Dove. Flower pure white ; central petals short, erect ; ray petals numerous, partly incurving.

Pigeon. Flower pale, delicate pink ; the disk petals strap shaped, very numerous and crowded ; ray petals few, reflexed.

Duck. Flower medium size ; white ; the ray petals in several rows.

Heron. Flower very large ; rosy pink ; ray petals in several rows.

20 cts. each, $2 per doz.

We will have ready for delivery on March 1st, all the Novelties of 1893. Please write for particulars and prices.

Our Collection of Seeds, Plants and Bulbs are of great value.

General Collection of Chrysanthemums Introduced in 1891.

This list contains the choicest of all the varieties introduced last year, all of which we have flowered.

Alberic Lunden. Rich crimson; recurved petals; large.
Anna. M. Weybrecht. Pure white petals; broad and solid.
Cesare Costa. Peculiar shade of red; large flowers.
Clara Reimer. White, with lavender markings; fine for pot-culture.
Chauncey Lloyd. Delicate, flesh-pink, shading to white; incurved, long, ray-like, sword petals.
Cleopatra. Chamois, shaded rose; broad petals.
Eldorado. Rich, deep yellow; incurved, broad petals, strong stems; keeps finely when cut.
Elmer D. Smith. Cardinal-red; back of petals clear chamois; large size.
Emily Dorner. Rich orange-yellow, touched with crimson; incurved petals; sturdy, dwarf grower.
Emma Dorner. Deep violet-pink, pure color; ball-shaped.
Flora Hill. Pure white; center creamy; heavy texture; one of the best.
Frank Thomson. White; pearly pink at base of petals; incurved; globular; fine.
Golden Gate. Bright yellow, reflexed petals; full center; fine.
John Firth. Soft, silvery pink; cup-shaped, built-up center.
John Goode. Outer petals delicate lavender; clear lemon center; globular; silky finish.
J. V. Farwell. Lavender without; inside of petals rosy violet; fine keeper.
Kate Rambo. Pure white, large flowers; petals slightly incurved at tips; distinct; a desirable sort.
King of Chrysanthemums. New seedling; incurved; broad petals; fine.
Lily Bates. Clear, bright pink; petals broad; distinct.
Lizzie Cartledge. Dark rose; reverse of petals silvery white; reflexed.
Louis Boehmer. Clear lilac incurved petals, feathered like those of Mrs. Alpheus Hardy, but a better flower and stronger grower. No collection is complete without it.
Massalia. Deep red; broad petals.
Mattie C. Stewart. Clear, bright yellow; broad, flat petals; reflexed.
M. Harry Laing. Light rose; golden center; tubular petals; very early.
Mikado. Bright, terra-cotta-red, light shadings; large and distinct.
Mme. Alfred Carriere. Milky white, globular flowers.
Mme. Camille Richard. Light rose; center old gold; large, imbricated flower.
Mme. Ed. Lefort. Reddish, laciniated petals, tipped with yellow.
Mme. Louise Langtos. Delicate lavender; dwarf grower; incurved.
Mme. Marie Mauvet. Deep yellow, shaded and spotted with red.
M. R. Owen. White, shaded rose; twisted petals; handsome flower.

LOUIS BOEHMER CHRYSANTHEMUM.

Mrs. D. D. L. Farson. Rich, silvery pink; large, compact forms.
Mrs. Frank Thomson. White, with pink markings; incurved, broad petals; immense size.
Mrs. I. D. Sailer. Soft, shell pink, incurved, sharply pointed petals, tipped with lemon; globular.
Mrs. Kendal. Rich, Jacqueminot-red; reverse of petals bronzy gold; compact center.
Mrs. R. J. Baylis. Clear yellow, marked with red, bronze and old gold; incurved; petals an inch wide; one of the largest.
Octa. Outer petals dashed with rose; center light yellow; incurved.
Prince of Chrysanthemums. Flesh-pink, incurved, tubular petals; beautiful.
Robert Flowerday. Upper surface of petals bright crimson-like; reverse silvery pink; large outer petals incurved.
Sabine Mea. Golden yellow, large, globular flowers.
Sec. Gen. Cassvigneau. White, shaded rose; large blooms.
Sugar Loaf. Varying shade of yellow, sometimes bronzy; outer petals recurve, center incurve; strong grower; free bloomer.
Vice Pres. Adignler. Soft, rose petals, tipped with white; very large, broad petals.
Williams White. Pure white; reflexed petals, full center.
Vonitza. White, tinted with green; perfect incurved; dense, built-up center.

Read what we say about Cannas, on page 3 of cover.

August Swanson. Bright scarlet, lined with old gold; fine for pots.

Robert Maitre. Clear, delicate pink; large and symmetrical; a good keeper when cut.

Mistletoe. Exterior of petals silvery white; crimson inner lining; broad petals; globular.

Mermaid. Delicate pink, incurved; daintily finished.

Anna Dorner. Rich carmine, striped and shaded, creamy white center; bold flower.

Leopard. Dark pink, curiously dotted with white; very distinct.

Sulphide. Yellow; incurved; fine grower and bloomer.

J. M. Jordan. Pure white; reflexed petals; large and fine.

Tyro. Light fawn color; high flower, broad petals; strong grower.

W. W. Lunt. Lemon-yellow; fine, large, massive flower.

Delaware. White; pale yellow anemone center; large and fine.

Jno. Dyer. Chrome yellow; petals striped with red lines; strong grower; flower of great substance.

Minerva. Light pink; single, needle-like, tubular petals; tips deeper.

Ulysses. Magenta; outside of petals deep lilac; incurving; large yellow eye.

Yellowstone Park. Clear yellow; reflexed petals; delicate, feathery form.

Pacific Wave. White, single; free bloomer; a fine flower.

Our Selection of 10, $2; or, 25 cents each.

General Collection of Chrysanthemums.

White Varieties.

Adirondack. Large white flowers, incurved; strong grower and free bloomer; a splendid variety.

Mrs. Alpheus Hardy. Pure white, incurved; reverse of petals thickly set with feathery-like hairs; very remarkable; a most beautiful flower.

Nymphæa. Pure white, sweet-scented; a novelty. Good for growing in pots.

Belle Poterine. White, incurved; very early.

Bride. White; incurved, drooping petals; one of the best.

Christmas Eve. Pure white, incurved; a good late variety.

Domination. Creamy white; good size.

Empress of Japan. White; long, graceful petals; incurved; large and beautiful.

International. Ivory-white; large and full.

Judge Rea. Pure white petals; yellow center.

L. Canning. Pure white; long, broad petals; free grower; one of the best.

Mme. Drexel. White, tinted with rose.

Mme. Louise Leroy. White; incurved, creamy center; free-flowering.

Marvel. White; maroon in center; a fine variety.

Miss Annie Hartshorn. Pure white; incurved, very large.

Miss M. Wanamaker. Creamy white, incurved; perfect ball; fine variety.

Mountain of Snow. Pure white; beautiful; fine for exhibition.

Molly Bawn. Pure white; triangular; beautiful.

Mrs. Langtry. Pure white; outside petals quilled; very large and beautiful flower.

Mrs. Sam. Houston. Pure white; incurved; large and fine.

Princess Teck. White, suffused with pink; incurved.

Pelican. Pure white; large, long, broad, curled florets; fine.

Williams, White. Pure white, reflexed petals, full center; one of the best.

HARRY E. WIDENER CHRYSANTHEMUM. (See page 66.)

Special prices will be quoted for large quantities.

Shades of Red Chrysanthemums.

Cullingfordii. Brilliant crimson, under side of petals old gold ; one of the finest.

E. W. Clark. Rich peony-red ; large and fine.

Mrs. Wm. Howells. Crimson, reflexed ; fine for pot culture.

Mrs. Carnegie. Velvety red ; incurved, large, broad petals.

Montezuma. Light red ; outer side of petals striped with gold ; yellow center.

Mrs. J. T. Emlin. Blood-red on upper side of petals; reverse old gold.

Montauk. Crimson-maroon ; flat petals, showing yellow center ; large.

Mrs. A. Haig. Dark red. large ; full in center.

Mrs. Wm. Bowen. Red and gold ; free grower and bloomer.

Mrs. George. Dark red ; good grower.

Ocrola. Bright red, reverse pale yellow ; twisted petals ; large, irregular flower.

Rothwell Hyde. Red, shaded with yellow ; large flower.

John Thorpe. Rich, deep lake ; long, broad petals, few tubular petals in under row ; flower large ; early bloomer and vigorous grower.

W. W. Coles. Terra cotta ; whorled center ; a popular variety.

Shades of Yellow.

Harry E. Widener. Pure, bright lemon-yellow ; incurved ; petals crisp and stiff ; long, erect stems ; flower averages 10 to 11 inches in diameter ; finest yellow for cut flowers.

Ramona. Bright amber ; incurved ; large and full ; petals or florets numerous ; long, slender and tubular.

Bettina. Clear orange ; long petals ; early, and lasts well.

California. Rich yellow ; incurved ; a perfect ball ; large, curly.

Comte de Germiny. Nankin-yellow ; large and novel.

Edwin H. Fittler. Brilliant yellow, slightly streaked with red ; large and fine.

Gold. Pure yellow ; flowers large ; fine for cutting in sprays.

Grandiflorum. Pure golden color ; petals broad, incurved ; solid ball ; fine variety.

Henry Cannell. Golden yellow ; incurved, ball-shaped ; strong.

John Collins. Yellow, orange shading ; large and full.

John Webster. Light orange.

Magicienne. Light lemon color ; tubular petals ; large, spreading flowers ; early.

Mrs. C. H. Wheeler. Orange-yellow, outside of petals crimson ; flower very large and heavy.

Miss Mary Weightman. Chrome-yellow ; loose, feathery form ; large and full.

Mrs. A. Waterer. Rich yellow, base of petals pink

Mrs. W. K. Harris. Rich chrome-yellow ; one of the finest yellows.

Suzon. Clear orange ; reflexed petals.

Source d'Or. Orange-gold shading ; twisted, reflexed petals.

Viele d'Or. Deep yellow ; fine, large flowers.

W. H. Lincoln. Golden yellow ; flat, spreading petals of great substance ; very large ; incurved.

Yellow Bird. Soft yellow ; long petals.

Shades of Pink.

Mrs. Irving Clarke. Margin of petals pearly white, shading to deep rose, center beautifully whorled ; large and fine.

Mrs. Levi P. Morton. Bright pink, base of petals white ; unique appearance ; should be in every collection.

Mrs. Fottler. Soft rose ; incurved, long-pointed petals ; large, and fine for cut-flowers.

Ada Spalding. Delicate shade of pink, incurved ; a beautiful flower.

Harman Payne. Deep rose ; very large flower ; long petals. Price, 25 cents each.

Excellent. Rosy pink ; large flower ; fine for cutting.

Elkhorn. Rich peach color ; incurved, segregated petals ; very fine.

Fred Hart. Flesh color ; incurved, large.

J. N Gerard. Pink ; one of the best of its color.

Lilian B. Bird. Beautiful shade of pink ; very large ; tubular petals ; one of the best.

Mrs. A. Blanc. Rich lavender ; inside florets erect ; strong grower.

Mrs. Mary Morgan. Soft blush ; beautiful, perfect flower.

Rose Queen. Bright rose ; a fine variety.

T. C. Price. Strawberry cream color ; petals twisted, incurved ; large.

10 cents each, or 12 for $1.

☞Chrysanthemums are a specialty with us, and we keep thoroughly posted on all the new varieties, as well as those suited for any special use. Therefore, we can give good service to any of our friends who are not familiar with the proper varieties, and will cheerfully make careful selections for any special purpose, or for general utility.

Bedding Plants.

These serve to brighten up the home grounds when planted in masses, and very fine decorative efforts can be attained by their judicious use. We do not list them separately with descriptions, but will have a select stock of the following varieties ready for shipping March 1 :

Ageratum, Alternanthera, Achyranthus, Alyssum, Begonias, Coleus, Dahlias, Fuchsias, Geraniums, Heliotropes, Hydrangeas, Lemon Verbena, Panicum, Petunias (Double and Single), Pelargoniums, Salvias, etc.

Prices from $1 to $2 per dozen, $6 to $15 per 100.

If you receive two Catalogues, give your neighbor one.

ORNAMENTAL DEPARTMENT.

Deciduous Trees.

AILANTUS (Tree of Heaven). A lofty, rapid-growing tree, with long, elegant, feathery foliage; useful for tropical effects; exempt from all diseases. 8 to 10 feet high, 50 cents each, ten for $4.

ALMOND, Large Double-flowering. A beautiful tree, covered with double, rose-colored blossoms, flowering in May. 8 to 10 feet high, 50 cents each, ten for $4.

BEECH, Purple-leaved. A vigorous and elegant tree; deep purple foliage in spring, changing to crimson later on. 3 to 4 feet high, $3 each.

CATALPA Kæmpferi. A Japanese variety, of medium growth, with deep green foliage; fragrant, cream-colored flowers. 8 to 10 feet high, 50 cents ten for each, ten for $4.

Speciosa. A hardy variety, originating in the western states; blooms earlier and is hardier than the common variety. 8 to 10 feet high, 50 cents each, ten for $4.

Syringæfolia. Wide-spreading head; large, pale green leaves, frequently six to seven inches wide; silvery bark; white flowers, marked with purple and yellow spots. 8 to 10 feet high, 50 cents each, ten for $4.

Bignonioides. Very similar to C. speciosa in growth; flowers darker in color. 50 cents each, ten for $4.

CHESTNUT, Spanish or Italian. It forms a handsome lawn tree; useful for ornament and fruit. 8 to 10 feet high, $1 each, ten for $7.50; 6 feet, 75 cents each, ten for $5; 4 feet, 50 cents each, ten for $4.

ELM, American, White. The noble spreading and drooping tree of our forest; strong growth, fine appearance. 8 to 10 feet high, 50 cents each, ten for $4; 6 to 8 feet, 40 cents each, ten for $3.50.

American, Black. Similar to the above, only more erect. 10 to 12 feet high, 75 cents each, ten for $6.

Cork-bark. This variety has proved itself to be the best shade tree for California, succeeding well in any soil; young branches very corky, in deep fissures. 10 to 12 feet high, 50 cents each, ten for $4.

English or French (Campestris). A rapid grower; lofty and very erect; leaves smaller and more regular than the American. 10 to 12 feet high, 50 cents each, ten for $4.

Latifolia. A quick grower, with broad leaves. 50 cents each.

Purple-leaved. Erect branches and purple leaves; very striking. 10 to 12 feet high, 75 cents each, ten for $6.

Variegated. Small leaves, with silvery spots; variegation constant. 8 to 10 feet high, 50 cents each, ten for $4.

HORSE-CHESTNUT, European or White-flowering. Very hardy, large-sized tree; regular outline; free from all diseases; magnificent, erect spikes of white flowers, marked lightly with red. 8 to 10 feet high, $1 each, ten for $7.50.

Red-flowering. Red flowers, and leaves deeper green than the European. 4 to 5 feet high, $1 each.

If you want a good Lawn, read page 2.

LABURNUM or Golden Chain. A beautiful tree, with long, drooping racemes of fragrant, yellow flowers. 4 to 6 feet high, 50 cents each, ten for $4.

LARCH, Japanese. The Money Pine of Japan. Very vigorous grower; dark, yellowish, ash-colored branches, and green foliage. 8 to 10 feet high, 75 cents each, ten for $6.

LINDEN, American. Very rapid grower; large leaves and fragrant flowers. 8 to 10 feet high, 75 cents each, ten for $6.

European. A fine pyramidal tree of large size; leaves large, and flowers fragrant. 10 to 12 feet high, $1 each.

White or Silver-leaved. A vigorous growing tree of pyramidal form; very conspicuous. 8 to 10 feet high, 75 cents each, ten for $6.

LOCUST, Common or Black. A well-known variety. 10 to 12 feet high, 35 cents each, ten for $2.50.

Inermis (Globe or Parasol Acacia). A very pretty tree; thornless, having a round, dense head, like a ball. 8 to 10 feet, $1 each.

Moss or Rose Acacia. A beautiful flowering variety from the southern states.

Rose-flowered. Branches gummy; rose colored flowers; very interesting. 3 feet high, 75 cts. each.

Thornless (*Bessoniana*). A noble and very ornamental tree; dark green foliage; entirely without thorns. 10 to 12 feet high, 50 cents each, ten for $4.

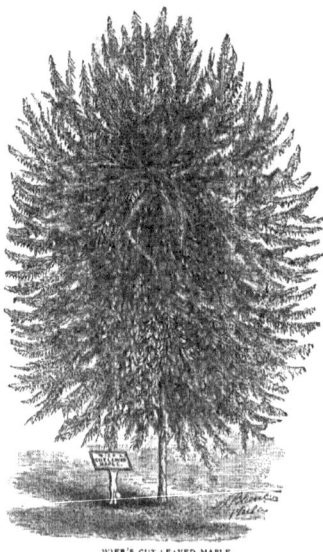

WIER'S CUT-LEAVED MAPLE.

LOCUST, Honey. A well-known tree, with powerful spines and delicate foliage. 2 to 3 feet high, 50 cents each, ten for $4.

MAGNOLIA acuminata (Cucumber Tree). A noble tree; leaves are large and flowers yellow; fruit resembles a cucumber when green. 4 to 5 feet high, $1 each.

Conspicua. Large, white flowers; full of fragrance. 3 to 4 feet high, $2 each.

Gracilis. Flowers reddish purple. 2 feet high, $1 each.

Purpurea. A small tree; flowers are dark purple, and cup-shaped. 2 to 2½ feet high, $1 each.

Rubra. A strong-growing variety; flowers deep red. 2 to 2½ feet high, $1 each.

Stellata. Similar to the American Water Lily; double white flowers.

MAIDEN-HAIR TREE (*Salisburia*). A native of Japan. Beautiful, fern-like foliage; rapid grower. 6 to 8 feet high, 75 cents each, ten for $4, 50 cents each, ten for $4.

MAPLE, Box Elder (*Negundo*). A good shade-tree; smaller than other Maples; a good grower; spreading form. 8 to 10 feet high, 30 cents each, ten for $2.50.

Variegated Box Elder (*Negundo Var.*). A very attractive and ornamental tree of dwarf habit; leaves distinctly marked with white. 6 to 8 feet high, 50 cents each, ten for $4.

Californica. A native of this state; growth upright and rapid. 3 to 4 feet high, 25 cents each, ten for $2.

English Cork-barked (*Campestre*). A stocky tree, of compact habit; handsome foliage; corky bark. 10 to 12 feet high, 60 cents each, ten for $5.

Norway. A noble and handsome tree; of rounded form; shining foliage; very desirable. 10 to 12 feet high, 60 cents each, ten for $5.

Oregon or Large-leaved. A very graceful variety; very large foliage and wide, spreading branches. 10 to 12 feet high, 60 cents each, ten for $5.

Purple-leaved. A fine specimen of robust habit; deep green foliage on the upper side, and purplish red underneath. 8 to 10 feet high, 60 cents each, ten for $5.

Silver or Soft. A native; very useful for avenue or park; a rapid grower; foliage silvery on the under side. 8 to 10 feet high, 50 cents each, ten for $4.

Sugar. A well-known variety of stately growth; fine form and foliage. 6 to 8 feet high, 75 cents each, ten for $6.

Sycamore. A handsome tree, also very rapid grower; large foliage; smooth, ash-gray bark. 8 to 10 feet high, 50 cents each, ten for $4.

Wier's Cut-leaved. A rapid grower; of graceful and drooping form of the Silver Maple. 8 to 10 feet high, 75 cents each, ten for $6.

MOUNTAIN ASH, European. A hardy tree, with dense and irregular head; blooms in July, with clusters of bright crimson berries. 8 to 10 feet high, 50 cents each, ten for $4.

Dwarf. A small, handsome tree. 50 cents each, ten for $4.

Oak-leaved. One of the finest of lawn trees; a very hardy tree; foliage simple and deeply cut. 4 to 6 feet high, 75 cents each, ten for $6.

MULBERRY, Russian. A rapid grower; bears young regularly; introduced by the Mennonite colonists of the northwest; fruit black and good. 8 to 10 feet high, 50 cents each, ten for $4.

Order now; don't wait until you are going to plant.

MULBERRY, White (*Morus alba*). Will grow anywhere when well established; is used for silk culture. 8 to 10 feet high, 25 cents each, ten for $2.

OAK, Water-oak (*Quercus aquatica*). Grows to forty feet in height; one of the finest of American Oaks. 6 to 8 feet, $1 each.

English (*Q. robur*). The Royal Oak of England. Majestic in maturity; very graceful when young. 10 to 12 feet high, 75 cents each, ten for $6.

Scarlet (*Q. coccinea*). A native, and rapid grower; very remarkable in autumn when the foliage changes to a bright scarlet color. 8 to 10 feet high, $1 each.

PAULOWNIA imperialis. A native of Japan; very magnificent; quick grower; it surpasses all others for size of leaves; large upright panicles of purple flowers in spring. 8 to 10 feet high, 75 cents each, ten for $6.

PECAN. A rapid-growing tree, producing valuable timber and heavy crops of oblong nuts; very beautiful and symmetrical. 4 to 5 feet high, 50 cents each, ten for $4.

PEACH, Double Crimson. A variety of Peach producing semi-double, bright red flowers in great abundance in early spring. 4 to 6 feet high, 50 cents each, ten for $4.

Double White. Similar to the Double Crimson, except that the flowers are white and double. 4 to 6 feet high, 50 cents each, ten for $4.

PERSIMMON, American. This is a well-known native variety, with smooth and glossy leaves; pale yellow flowers and reddish yellow fruit. 6 to 8 feet high, 75 cents each, ten for $5.

European. A noble tree; foliage dark, glossy green above, and downy underneath. 6 to 8 feet high, 75 cents each.

POPLAR, Carolina. Large leaves; very rapid growth. 10 to 12 feet high, 40 cts. each, ten for $3.

Lombardy. Very erect and of spire-like form; quick grower; a native of Italy. 8 to 10 feet high, 40 cents each, ten for $3.

White or Silver. A wonderfully rapid grower; has a wide-spreading habit; large leaves, green above and snow-white beneath. 8 to 10 feet high, 40 cents each, ten for $3.

SYCAMORE, European. A straight-growing tree; very clean, and grows entirely free from mildew; is planted on the boulevards of Paris. 10 to 12 feet high, 75 cents each, ten for $5.

TAMARIX. A beautiful small tree, foliage somewhat resembling that of Juniper; delicate, small flowers; will thrive anywhere. 4 to 6 feet high, 30 cents each, ten for $2.50.

TEXAS UMBRELLA. This tree has a dense, spreading head, resembling an umbrella; very sweet flowers; very popular in the southern states as a shade tree. 7 to 8 feet, $1 each.

THORN, English Hawthorn (*Oxyacantha*). Makes a good hedge; flowers single and showy; nice perfume. 4 to 5 feet high, 40 cents each, ten for $3.

FRUIT OF RUSSIAN MULBERRY. (See page 68.)

THORN, Double White. Very ornamental variety, as regards both foliage and flowers; flowers double white. 4 to 6 feet high, 50 cents each.

TULIP TREE (*Liriodendron*). A handsome native variety; leaves broad and fiddle-shaped; flowers yellow, tulip-shaped. 4 to 5 feet high, 75 cents each; 3 to 4 feet, 50 cents each.

VIRGILIA lutea (Yellow Wood). A fine specimen, with broadly rounded and compact head; leaves similar to the Locust; white flowers like pea-blossoms; very fragrant. 4 to 6 feet high, $1 each.

WALNUT, American Black. One of the best and largest of American forest trees; the wood it produces is very valuable; it grows freely on this coast, and stands transplanting well. 8 to 10 feet high, 75 cents each, ten for $5.

California Black. This variety makes an excellent shade tree; a very rapid grower in any soil; bears a nut with a hard shell. 8 to 10 feet high, 50 cents each, ten for $4.

WILLOW, Golden. Very conspicuous at all times, especially in winter, on account of its yellow bark; very handsome. 6 to 8 feet high, 25 cents each, ten for $2.

Osier or Basket. Has long, slender shoots; low-growing. 6 to 8 feet high, 25 cents each, ten for $2.

Ring-leaved. A good growing variety; upright; its branches retain their weeping habit; small foliage, dark green and curiously curled. 35 cts. each.

Sallow (*Caprea*). A small tree; blooms very early, producing its short, silky catkins before the leaves. 35 cents each.

XANTHOCERAS Sorbifolia. Very hardy and beautiful; of small stature; leaves like the Mountain Ash; white flowers, with a purple eye. 1 foot high, 75 cents each.

Deciduous Weeping Trees.

ASH, European Weeping. Very useful for lawn or arbor. A well-known variety; rapid grower. $1 each.

Gold-barked Weeping. An elegant weeping tree; bark in winter as yellow as gold, and very conspicuous on the lawn. $1 each.

BIRCH, Cut-leaved Weeping. Without a doubt the most elegant of all weeping trees. Its silver-white bark, drooping branches and delicately cut foliage present a very attractive appearance, and it is a great favorite. $1 each.

Young's Weeping. A very useful variety, of a more compact habit. $1 each.

LABURNUM, Weeping. Produces a fine effect. $1 each.

MULBERRY, Teas' Weeping Russian. This tree is without a rival; its branches droop till they touch the ground. It is one of the most graceful of hardy weeping trees. $1.50 each.

WILLOW, American Weeping. One of the dwarf slender species. It makes one of the most ornamental of small weeping trees, when grafted five or six feet high. $1 each.

Kilmarnock. A very graceful tree. It has a glossy foliage and perfect, umbrella-like head. Very charming for lawns. $1 each.

Common (Babylonica). The well-known Weeping Willow. 50 cents each.

Lick's. A beautiful weeper. It is a cross between the common Weeping Willow and the Black California Willow. 35 cents each, 10 for $2.50.

Evergreen Trees and Shrubs.

ACACIA. The Acacias are a beautiful class of trees, as they flower in winter and early spring, when few other trees are in bloom.

Dealbata. Fine, feathery foliage; one of the best. 50 cents each.

Decurrens. A handsome variety, with fine, feathery foliage. 50 cents each.

Floribunda. Rapid grower; of pendulous habit; flowers profusely when quite young. 50 cts. each.

Latifolia. A moderate-sized tree, with fine foliage. 50 cents each.

Melanoxylon. A fine, symmetrical tree; very useful for street planting. 50 cents each, ten for $4.

ARAUCARIA Bidwellii. A handsome lawn tree; most majestic; spiny, shining, deep green leaves; perfectly hardy. $6 each.

Imbricata (Chili Pine). Beautiful, pyramidal form; leaves stiff, smooth, deep green, and sharply pointed, entirely clothing the branchlets. $8, $6, $4 and $3 each.

ARAUCARIA.

ARBOR-VITÆ, Chinese Variegated. Very erect grower; splendid foliage. $1 each.

Golden (Aurea). This variety is well known; conical form. $1.50 each.

Elegantissima. A beautiful, pyramidal tree; foliage grand. $1 to $2 each.

Ever-Golden (Semper aurea). Similar to Elegantissima. One of the best of its variety. $1 each.

Gigantea or Lobbii. This tree attains a great size, and is very ornamental. It has numerous slender branchlets, and is a very rapid grower. $1 each.

ARBUTUS Unedo. A handsome shrub; blooms in winter, having red berries at the same time. Native of Spain and Italy. $1 each.

AUCUBA Japonica. A beautiful shrub. It has large, shining, gold-blotched leaves; requires shade. $1, 75 cents and 50 cents each.

BAMBOO, Falcata. This tree grows 20 feet high, and is very ornamental, having young shoots, long and graceful, like fishing rods. 50 cents each, ten for $3.50.

Metake. A dwarf variety, having large leaves, and growing about 7 feet high, with erect, tufty stems; the branches are also erect; dark green leaves. 50 cents each, ten for $3.50.

Viridis striata. A native of Japan; a vigorous grower, also hardy. It has long, green leaves on both sides, with yellowish and deep green bands; one of the best. 50 cents each, ten for $3.50.

BERBERIS Darwinii. The finest of all Berberis; foliage small, thick and leathery; flowers orange-yellow and full of fragrance. 75 cents each.

Dulcis (Sweet-fruited Barberry). Medium size; flowers bright yellow; berries round, black. 50 cents each.

BOX TREE. Most useful and ornamental; it will grow under other trees and in the shade, and can be pruned into any shape or form. 50 cents each. The following are fine varieties:

Golden Variegated. 3 to 4 feet high. 75 cents each.

Silver Variegated. 2 to 3 feet high. 50 cts. each.

Hansworth. 2 to 2½ feet high. 50 cents each.

Dwarf (Suffruticosa). Makes a fine edging, and is used extensively. $4 per 100.

BROOM, Scotch. A very profuse flowering shrub in May and June. 50 cents to $1 50 each.

CALIFORNIA BAY TREE (Oreodaphne). A native of California; very rapid grower, with light green foliage, which emits an agreeable perfume. 12 inches high, 50 cents.

CALIFORNIA BIG TREE (Sequoia gigantea). The famous big tree of California. $1 to $3 each.

We will send ten varieties California Tree Seeds for One Dollar.

CALIFORNIA NUTMEG (Torreya). A handsome, yew-like tree; grows from 20 to 40 feet high, and forms a compact, rounded head. 4 to 6 ft. high, $2 ea.

CALIFORNIA RED-BERRY, or California Holly. This beautiful tree will grow almost anywhere, and yield its wealth of bright red berries for Christmas decorations. 50 cents each.

CAMELLIA Japonica. A beautiful winter flowering shrub. To grow them with success in the open ground, a little care must be taken, and they must be shaded the first season after planting. The following are fine varieties:
Double White. 2 to 3 feet high, $2 each.
"   Pink. 2 to 3 feet high, $2 each.
"   Red. 2 to 3 feet high, $2 each.
Variegated. Red, striped white. $2 each.

CAMPHOR TREE (*Laurus Camphora*). A valuable Japanese tree. The young growth appears in a most beautiful shade of red and purple. It has a very strong odor of camphor, and from the small branchlets and roots camphor is obtained by distillation. 3 to 4 feet high, 75 cents; ten for $6.

CEDAR, Deodar or Indica. An exceedingly handsome tree, of graceful, drooping habit; vigorous grower; foliage light silvery or glaucous green. 8 to 10 feet high, $8 each; 3 to 4 feet high, $3; 2 to 3 feet high, $2.
Lebanon. Strong grower; wide-spreading, horizontal branches; dark green foliage. 6 to 7 feet high, $6 each; 5 to 6 feet high, $4 each.

CEPHALOTAXUS Fortunei. A handsome tree, native of Japan; dark green foliage and long, slender, drooping branches. 2 to 2½ ft. high, $1 ea.
Drupacea. A small evergreen tree, succeeding best in moist, shady places; very attractive; fruit purple. 2 to 2½ feet high, $1 each.

CHOISYA ternata. A beautiful, free-growing shrub; a profuse bloomer; flowers pure white; sweet-scented. 75 cents each.

CRYPTOMERIA Japonica (*Japan Cedar*). Presents a fine appearance, growing 50 to 60 feet high; from China and Japan. 3 to 4 feet high, $1 each.

CYPRESS Guadalupensis. An erect and strong grower; foliage of a bluish cast. 50 cents each.
Funeral (*Funebris*). A noble species, with forked branches, dividing into numerous pendulous branchlets. 3½ to 4 feet high, 50 cents each.
Italian. A tall, tapering, conical tree, planted extensively in cemeteries. 6 to 8 ft. high, 75 cents ea.
Lawson. A beautiful native tree; drooping, feathery branches. 3 to 4 feet high. $1 each.
Monterey. A well-known variety, planted extensively in California; useful for hedges. 2 to 3 feet high, ten for $2.

DAPHNE, White-flowering. A medium-sized shrub; foliage deep green; flowers very fragrant. 2 to 3 feet high. $1.50 each.
Variegated. Flowers purplish. 1½ to 2 feet high, $1.50 each.

ESCALLONIA Sanguinea. Bright red flowers. 3 to 4 feet high, 75 cents each.

EUONYMUS Japonica. Bright green, glossy leaves. 2½ to 3 feet high, 35 cents each.
Aurea. Golden-leaved.
Latifolia aurea marginata. Leaves edged yellow. 2 to 3 feet high, 50 cents each.
Radicans variegata. A creeping variety; foliage silver edged. 1 to 2 feet high, 35 cents each.

EUCALYPTUS, Blue Gum (*Globulus*). A well-known tree. 4 to 5 ft. high, 25 cents ea.; ten for $2.
Red Gum (*Rostrata*). A rapid-growing variety of the Australian Gum Tree. 4 to 5 feet high, 25 cents each; ten for $2.
We also grow a few of the following Eucalypti: *Corymbosa, Hermastroma, Leucoxylon, Longifolia, Obliqua, Paniculata, Sideraphloia, Tereticornis.* Blue Gums, in boxes, 2 years, $25 per 1,000.

FILARIA laurifolia. Very handsome; of quite recent introduction; small, leathery leaves. 4 to 5 feet high, $1 each.

GREVILLEA ROBUSTA.

GREVILLEA robusta. A beautiful, rapid-growing variety; dark green foliage and orange-colored flowers. $1, 75 cents and 50 cents each.

HOLLY, European. A beautiful small tree; a good grower, and covered during the winter with red berries. 1½ to 2 feet high, $1.50 each.
Variegated Varieties. The growth is similar to the European; leaves beautifully marked with yellow and white; valuable as lawn plants. 1 to 2 feet high, $3 each.

JUNIPER, Irish. A distinct variety; very upright growth, with glaucous green foliage. 2 to 2½ feet high, $1 each.
Japan. Foliage similar to the Irish. It is very handsome; a native of China and Japan. 2 to 2½ feet high, $1 each.

LAUREL, English. Broad, green foliage; creamy white flowers, succeeded by large purple berries. 3 to 4 feet high, 75 cents each.
Latifolia. A variety of English Laurel; foliage extremely deep green; leaves grow to a foot long. 3 to 4 feet high, 75 cents each.
Portugal. A very compact shrub; flowers similar to the English. 2 to 3 feet high, 75 cents each.
Nobilis (*Sweet Bay*). Very ornamental leaves, and berries; very fragrant. 6 to 7 feet high, $1.50; 10 to 12 inches high, 50 cents.

LAURUSTINUS. The handsomest of all winter shrubs; flowers white, in clusters; very profuse bloomer.

LIGUSTRUM coriaceum. A handsome dwarf variety, with leathery leaves and large white flowers. 2 to 3 feet high, 40 cents each; ten for $3.50, ten for $25.
Japanese. A large shrub, with leathery, dark green, glossy leaves and white flowers. 75 cts. ea.

LOQUAT. An ornamental tree; foliage dark green; fragrant white flowers, and produces a tart, yellow, edible fruit. 50 and 75 cents each.

MADRONO. A native of this coast; large, thick foliage and fragrant white flowers, succeeded by red berries. 18 to 24 inches high, $1 each.

Johnson Grass is the best forage plant grown.

CEDAR DEODORA.

MAGNOLIA grandiflora. The most beautiful of all American Evergreens. No garden is complete without it. This variety is well known. 6 to 8 feet high, $3; 10 for $25; 4 to 5 feet high, $2 each.

Olouiensis. Fine double-flowered variety; very free bloomer. 4 to 5 ft. high, $5; 2 to 3 ft. $3 each.

MAHONIA aquifolium. A native variety, with purplish, shiny, prickly leaves; flowers bright yellow, succeeded by bluish berries. 3 to 4 feet high, $1 each.

Bealii. A very distinct species; leaves about a foot long, of a yellowish green tint. 1 to 1½ ft. high, $1.

Japonica. Nearly similar to Bealii. 2 to 3 feet high, $1 each.

MYRTLE. A dwarf shrub; fragrant leaves and white flowers. 50 cents to $1 each.

OLEANDER. One of the most profuse blooming evergreens, flowering from May to November. Should be planted in a full exposure to the sun, which serves to keep them healthy and aids their blooming. 50 cents each, ten for $4.

Lillian Henderson. Flower white, flat and double. 75 cents to $1 each.

Madoni grandiflora. The best white Oleander; strong grower; flowers semi-double. 75 cents to $1 each.

Purpurea grandiflorum. Deep rose-colored flowers. 75 cents each.

Common Single White. 50 cents each.

PINE, Austrian. A strong, spreading tree; leaves dark and stiff. 3 to 4 feet high, 75 cents each.

Benthamiana (Bentham's Pine). One of the finest of pines, attaining a height of over 200 feet, with irregular branches and deep green leaves. 1 to 2 feet high, $1 each.

PINE, Canariensis. Quick growing; very handsome. 4 to 5 feet high, $1.50 each.

Jeffreyii. Very hardy and of much value, with deep, beautiful green leaves. 4 to 5 feet high, $1 each.

Mediterranean. A beautiful tree, of erect habit. 2 to 3 feet high, 75 cents each.

Monterey. Our well-known native variety; very handsome, and can be seen anywhere. 4 to 5 feet high, 50 cents each.

Muricata. One of the small varieties; very handsome. 4 to 5 feet high, 75 cents each.

Ponderosa. A colossal variety, with few branches; wood very heavy when cut. 4 to 5 feet high, $1 each.

Sabiniana. A large, noble tree, with foliage of a silvery gray color. 6 to 12 inches high, 50 cents each.

Tuberculata. A handsome, medium-sized tree, with stiff, bright green foliage. 50 cents each.

PITTOSPORUM nigricans. A large, beautiful shrub, of rapid growth; foliage light green color; a valuable lawn tree. 1 to 1½ feet high, 75 cents each.

Tobira. A dense, low, spreading shrub; dark green foliage; flowers white and fragrant. 2 to 3 feet high, 50 cents.

REDWOOD (*Sequoia sempervirens*). A rapid-growing variety; very valuable for its timber. 35 to 75 cents each.

RHODODENDRON Ponticum. A fine, large shrub; flowers pale purplish violet, spotted. From $1 to $3 each.

SPRUCE, Douglas. A magnificent tree, of very rapid growth, attaining a great height —sometimes 300 feet. 4 to 6 ft. high, $1.50 ea.

Grandis. A very majestic tree; leaves apple-green above, silvery beneath; very distinct; reaches in height 200 feet. 4 to 5 feet high, $1.50 each.

Menzies. Similar to White Spruce in form and habit; foliage rich blue color. 2 to 2½ feet high, $1.50 each.

Nobilis. A symmetrical tree; spreading branches; foliage bluish green. 1½ to 2 feet high, $2 each.

Nordmann's Silver. A majestic variety of recent introduction; growth slow, but eventually becomes large; branches horizontal; foliage massive, dark green, silvery underneath; the contrast in color between the old and new growth is most charming. 1 to 1½ feet high, $2.50 each.

Norway (*Excelsa*). A compact and symmetrical tree, the branches assuming a graceful, drooping habit with age. 50 cents $2 each.

THUYOPSIS Dolobrata. Axe-leaved Arbor-vitæ; a peculiar tree from Japan; a vigorous grower; drooping branches, and leaves quite flattened and distinctly marked with rich golden yellow. $1 ea.

VERONICA Andersonii. One of the best evergreen flowering shrubs; flowers violet-blue. 35 cents each.

Variegated. A very handsome shrub; blue flowers. 35 cents each.

YEW, English. Large bush; very bushy head; can be trimmed into any shape. 4 to 5 ft. high, $1 ea.

Erect, English. An erect, dense-growing variety, with small, dark, thickly set leaves. 4 to 5 feet high, $1 each.

Golden. The foliage of this variety in June is of a rich golden hue; unsurpassed by any other variegated evergreens. 1½ to 2 feet high, $2.50 each.

Irish. Peculiarly upright in growth; the foliage is of the darkest hue, and the whole plant appears like a deep green column. $2 to $3 each.

Deciduous Flowering Shrubs.

ALTHEA or Rose of Sharon. The Altheas are fine, free-growing, free-flowering shrubs of the easiest cultivation, and are particularly desirable on account of blooming in August and September, when very few other trees or shrubs are in bloom; 3 to 4 feet high, 50 cents each, ten for $4. The following are the best varieties:

Bicolor hybrida. Flowers white and red; double. 3 to 4 feet high, 50 cents each, ten for $4.

Carnea plena. Flowers flesh color; large and double. 3 to 4 feet high, 50 cents each, ten for $4.

Monstrosa. Very large, double flowers. 3 to 4 feet high, 50 cents each, ten for $4.

Speciosa. White. 3 to 4 feet high, 50 cents each, ten for $4.

Variegated. Very showy and distinct variety; foliage handsome; flowers double purple. 3 to 4 feet high, 50 cents each, ten for $4.

ALMOND. Dwarf, double-flowering shrubs, producing in the greatest profusion finely formed flowers, making one mass of bloom. We cultivate the two best varieties, viz.: Double White and Double Pink. 3 to 4 four feet high, 50 cts each.

AZALEA Mollis. Red-salmon and yellow flowers; a beautiful spring-flowering plant of easy culture.

BERBERRY, Purple-leaved. An interesting shrub, with violet-purple foliage and fruit. 3 to 4 feet high, 50 cents each.

CALYCANTHUS or Sweet Shrub. Rich foliage and fragrant wood; flowers double purple and very fragrant. 3 to 4 feet high, 35 cents each.

Occidentalis (California Sweet Shrub). A larger growing shrub than the Sweet Shrub, and having inodorous flowers. 1 to 2 feet high, 50 cents each.

CORCHORUS, Silver Variegated. A compact-growing shrub; leaves edged with white; flower yellow. 1 to 2 feet high, 35 cents each.

CURRANT, Crimson-flowering. Deep red flower in spring. 6 to 8 feet high, 75 cents each.

Double Rose. Double flowers. 2 to 3 feet high, 50 cents each.

DEUTZIA. Fine, hardy shrubs; they are beautiful and popular, and easy to cultivate; the flowers are produced in racemes four to six inches long.

Crenata. White flowers, tinged with pink; a most desirable shrub. 40 cents each.

Crenata flora pleno. Abundant racemes of double, pure white flowers. 40 cents each.

Flora plena. Flowers double; white, tinged with pink; very desirable. 40 cents each.

Gracilis. A charming species; compact habit; flowers pure white and double. 40 cents each.

CALYCANTHUS.

Scabra. Rough-leaved; one of the most beautiful white flowering shrubs. 40 cents each.

DOGWOOD, Red-twigged. A native variety; very conspicuous in winter, when the bark is blood-red; flowers also beautiful in spring. 2 to 3 feet high, 40 cents each.

Variegated-leaved. Desirable for its foliage; a large spreading shrub; flowers white. 1 foot high, $1.50 each.

ELDER, Cut-leaved. A fine, large shrub; the leaves curiously and beautifully divided. 6 to 8 feet high, 50 cents each.

Golden-leaved. One of the best of its class; has solid golden leaves; very effective among other plants for the beautiful contrast it affords. 2 to 3 feet high, 75 cents each.

Variegated. A healthy grower; foliage splendidly mottled with white and yellow. 3 to 4 feet high, 40 cents each.

ERYTHRINA crista galli (Coral Plant). This plant is most valuable for bedding, being hardy in any climate; flowers dark crimson. 3 to 4 feet high, $1 each.

EUONYMUS or Spindle Tree. Green foliage and red berries; very desirable shrub. 5 to 7 feet high, 50 cents each.

FILBERT, Purple-leaved. Dark purple leaves; very conspicuous, and an excellent shrub. 1 to 2 feet high, 50 cents each.

FORSYTHIA or Golden Bell. Very useful small shrubs, with drooping, yellow flowers, which appear before the leaves. 2 to 3 feet high, 25 cents each.

Fortunei. Upright growth; deep green foliage. 2 to 3 feet high, 25 cents each.

Suspensa. Growth somewhat drooping. 2 to 3 feet high, 25 cents each.

Viridissima. Leaves and bark dark green; flowers a deep yellow, produced in early spring before the leaves; one of the best early shrubs. 2 to 3 feet high, 25 cents each.

Try a packet of Perpetual-flowering Pelargoniums.

HYDRANGEA PANICULATA.

HYDRANGEA paniculata. Panicle-flowered Hydrangea. A fine shrub, growing from eight to ten feet high; flowers white, in great pyramidal panicles a foot long, and produced in August and September, when very few shrubs are in flower; one of the finest flowering shrubs in California. 1 to 2 feet high, 50 cents each.

Thos. Hogg. This belongs to the Hortensis section of the family, but is a far more free and abundant bloomer than any other; for the florist and all decorative purposes it is invaluable; the flowers are of the purest white, of very firm texture, and are produced from July to September. 50 cents each.

Otaksa. Foliage a beautiful deep green color; the plant produces immense trusses of rose-colored flowers in profusion, in July, free-blooming. 50 cents each.

Hortensis. Garden or Changeable Hydrangea. Native of Japan, introduced in 1790. An elegant, well-known plant, with large leaves and large, globular heads of rose-colored flowers; usually grown in pots or boxes; in the north it requires protection out of doors in winter. 50 cents each.

LEMON VERBENA. A shrub well-known for its fragrant leaves; indispensable in the formation of bouquets. 25 cents each.

LILAC. Large, hardy-growing shrub; attractive foliage, with clusters of early, fragrant flowers.

Josikea. Upright shape; flowers deep lilac in June; very choice. 2 to 3 feet high, 50 cents each.

Persian Cut-leaved. Foliage elegantly cut; purple flowers. 3 to 4 feet high, 50 cents each.

LILAC, Purple. The common variety. A good grower; flowers very fragrant. 4 to 5 feet high, 75 cents each.

Sanguinea. Vigorous grower; a fine species. 4 to 5 feet high, 50 cents each.

White. Cream colored flowers. 4 to 5 feet high, 50 cents each.

MOCK ORANGE (*Philadelphus*). A very valuable shrub; handsome foliage and beautiful white flowers; vigorous habit. 3 to 4 feet high, 25 cents each.

Coronarius. Pure white, highly-scented flowers. 3 to 4 feet high, 25 cents each.

Dianthiflorus, fl. pl. A dwarf variety; flowers double, and cream color; very fragrant. 75 cents each.

Grandiflorus. Large flowers; very showy. 75 cents each.

PRUNUS pseudo-cerasus (Flowering Cherry). One of the finest flowering trees, having immense clusters of pure white flowers. $1 each

PLUM, Double-flowering (*Triloba*). A very desirable shrub; flowers a delicate pink, double, and set closely on tne slender branches.

Purple-leaved (*Pissardi*). A very promising new variety; foliage deep purple throughout the summer. 50 cents to $1 each.

PURPLE FRINGE, Smoke-Tree (*Rhus Cotinus*). A shrub admired by all; it has a curious fringe or hair-like flowers. 4 to 5 feet high, 50 cents each.

There may be something in our Plant Department that you are looking for.

POMEGRANATE, Double White. A fine, free-flowering shrub, with abundant double, creamy white flowers. 3 to 4 feet high, 40 cents each.
Double Red. Flowers double scarlet; a very beautiful small tree. 2 to 3 feet high, 40 cents each.
Dwarf. Free-bloomer, even when very small; flowers orange-scarlet, very brilliant; very desirable as a hedge plant. 2 to 3 feet high, 40 cents each.

QUINCE. The following varieties of the Japan Quince rank among our choicest shrubs. They are one mass of flowers in spring.
Japan Scarlet. Bright crimson-scarlet flowers. 3 to 4 feet high, 40 cents each.
Japan White. A very beautiful variety; delicate white and blush flowers. 2 to 3 feet high, 40 cents each.

SNOWBALL. A favorite shrub with every one; large size; flowers pure white, in large, globular clusters. 3 to 4 feet high, 50 cents each.

SPIRÆA. This comprises a large class of elegant shrubs of very easy culture. They bloom throughout the summer. 40 cents each.
Billardi. Rose-colored.
Callosa. Large panicles of deep rosy blossoms.

SPIRÆA VAN HOUTTEI.

SYMPHORICARPUS (Snowberry). A well-known variety; has small, pink flowers, followed by large white berries, which hang on the bush through part of the winter. 50 cents each.

VIBURNUM Plicatum (Japan Snowball). An improvement on the common variety; of moderate growth; plicated leaves; globular heads of pure white, neutral flowers. $1 each.
Macrocephalum. A Japanese variety, with very large flowers. $1.50 each.

WEIGELIA. Produces from April to June superb, large, trumpet shaped flowers of all shades and colors from pure white to red. From Japan. 35 cents each, except where noted.
Abel Carriere. Deep red.
Candida. A valuable new variety; flowers pure white.
Hendersonii. Deep rose-colored flowers.
Hortensis Nivea. Flowers snow-white; good bloomer.
Lavallei. The darkest variety; dark, reddish flowers.
Nana variegata. One of the best dwarf, variegated shrubs; foliage silver, variegated; stands the sun well.
Rosea. An elegant shrub; fine rose-colored flowers.
Van Houttei. Carmine.
Variegata elegans. New; foliage beautifully variegated. 50 cents each.

JAPAN QUINCE.

Callosa alba. Habit dwarf and bushy; white flowers.
Lanceolata. Flowers white and showy; early bloomer.
Prunifolia fl. pl. This variety is well-known as the Bridal Wreath; flowers double.
Reevesii flore pleno. A beautiful double-flowering variety.
Semperflorens. Upright grower; long spikes of white flowers.
Thunbergii. Light, yellowish green foliage; delicate, drooping; abundance of white flowers.
Van Houttei. Profusely covered in April with white flowers.

SUMACH, Cut-leaved. A very striking plant; leaves very large, deeply cut, drooping gracefully from the branches, and turning to a rich red in autumn. 3 to 4 feet high, 50 cents each.

POMEGRANATE, DOUBLE.

We can Guarantee Satisfaction, because we Know what we Sell.

HARDY VINES & CREEPERS

AKEBIA Quinata. A beautiful climber from Japan, with neat, small, sub-evergreen leaves, purple flowers and ornamental fruit. 50 cents each.

AMPELOPSIS Veitchii (Japan Ivy). From Japan; leaves smaller than *Akebia quinata* and overlap one another, forming a dense sheet of green. 50 cents each.

Quinquefolia (American Ivy). A fine specimen for covering verandas, walls, etc; a rapid climber. 35 cents each; ten for $2.

CLEMATIS. These are perfectly hardy, and one of the best of climbers; the flowers are beautiful, and are of various colors; the foliage is good; it is also a rapid grower, and will climb in any position.

Belle of Woking. Bluish mauve, or silver gray. $1 each.

Duchess of Edinburgh. The best of the double pure whites; deliciously scented. June and July. $1 each.

Gypsy Queen. Bright, dark, velvety purple; July to October. 75 cents each.

Guiding Star. Purplish, shaded crimson. July to October. 75 cents each.

Henryi. Large, finely formed; of a beautiful, creamy white. July to October. 75 cents each.

Jackmanni. One of the best varieties; intense violet-purple. June to November. 75 cents each.

Lanuginosa candida. Tinted grayish white. July to November. 75 cents each.

Lord Derby. Pale lavender, or delicate bluish lilac; flowers are red at the base, with white filaments. April to June. 75 cents each.

Purpurea elegans. Deep violet-purple. July to October. 75 cents each.

Standishii. Light mauve-purple. July to October. 75 cents each.

The Queen. Lavender, or mauve-lilac tint; flowers primrose-scented and six inches across; beautiful. May and June. $1 each.

William Kennet. Deep lavender. July to October. 75 cents each.

DUTCHMAN'S PIPE (*Aristolochia*). A vigorous climber; foliage light green, heart-shaped; flowers yellowish brown, curiously pipe-shaped. 50 cents each.

HONEYSUCKLE, Belgian. Flowers red and yellow; very fragrant; blooms all summer. 25 cents each.

Fuchsioides. Brilliant, scarlet flowers; one of the finest. 25 cents each.

Sempervirens. Flowers scarlet; blooms all summer. 25 cents each.

Sinensis. A well-known variety; very fragrant; holds its foliage very late. July and September. 25 cents each.

Variegata. Flowers fragrant; leaves handsomely marked. 25 cents each.

IVY, Giant. Very hardy, with large, thick, leathery leaves. 50 cents each.

Irish. Large, dark green, luxuriant leaves. 50 cents each.

Variegated. Leaves green and yellowish white. 50 cents each.

JASMINE, Catalonian. Flowers pure white, double, and deliciously fragrant. 50 cents each.

Nudiflorum. Numerous yellow leaves. From November through the winter. 50 cents each.

Officinale. White flowers; very fragrant; delicate, beautiful foliage; hardy. 25 cents each.

MANDEVILLEA Suaveolens (Chile Jasmine). Beautiful white flowers; a graceful climber. 50 cents each.

SILK VINE (*Periploca*). A rapid climber, with glossy foliage and clusters of purplish brown flowers. 35 cents each.

TRUMPET VINE (*Bignonia*). A well-known climber; flowers orange-scarlet and trumpet-shaped; one of the finest hardy climbers. 25 cents each.

VIRGINIA CREEPER. (See Ampelopsis.)

WISTARIA magnifica. Flowers in dense, drooping racemes, of a pale lilac; foliage very graceful. 50 cents each.

White. Pure white flowers, in long, pendulous clusters; rapid climber; attains a great size. 75 cents each.

Purple. Flowers pale blue; a fine variety of this grand climber. 50 cents each.

Double Purple. Double flowers in dense racemes, about the same length as the purple. 75 cts. each;

SHERWOOD HALL NURSERY CO.'S VIOLET BEDS AT MENLO PARK.

Herbaceous Bedding and Border Plants.

ANEMONE Japonica Alba (Honorine Joubert). Fine, large flowers, produced very freely in autumn. 25 cents each.

ARMERIA (Sea Pink, Thrift). A satisfactory border plant; narrow, grass-like leaves; rose colored flowers on long stems. 15 cents each.

ARUNDINARIA (Variegated Ribbon Grass). Handsomely striped foliage; one of the prettiest. 25 cents each.

ARUNDO Donax variegata. A tall, graceful plant, with ribbon-like foliage, beautifully striped. 50 cents each.

CLEMATIS erecta. Large panicles of fragrant white flowers, on stems 3 to 4 feet high. 25 cts. ea.

EULALIA Japonica variegata. A distinct grass from Japan with graceful stems four feet high, which are crowned, when fully ripe, with light mosses, presenting the appearance of ostrich feathers. 50 cents each.

Japonica Zebrina. Similar to the preceding. 50 cents each.

LARKSPUR (*Delphinium Formosum*). A very showy plant, producing magnificent spikes of dark blue flowers; very desirable. 25 cents each.

LILY OF THE VALLEY. Clumps, 50 cents.

NEW ZEALAND FLAX (*Phormium Tenax*). Very ornamental, large, flag-like leaves. $1 each.
Variegated. Handsomely variegated. $1 each.

PAMPAS GRASS. The best ornamental grass in cultivation; it has large plumes from 8 to 10 feet high; when properly dried makes a handsome parlor ornament. 50 cents each.

PÆONY, Herbaceous. Without a doubt one of the most beautiful ornaments. Their extremely large and showy flowers of various colors, their rich and glossy foliage and easy culture, are important arguments in favor of their extensive cultivation. In our collection will be found the best and most distinct sorts. Write for prices.

PÆONY (Tree). Most beautiful for border planting; 25 distinct varieties. Write for prices.

PLUMBAGO Capensis. A showy herbaceous plant; flowers in large trusses, light blue; climbing habit. 25 cents each.

TRITOMA uvaria (Poker Plant). Splendid winter-flowering plant; flowers red and orange. 25 cents each.

VIOLETS. These are a specialty with us, and we grow them in large quantities with great success.

Marie Louise. Very large, double, fragrant flowers; lavender, blue and white.

Neapolitan. Large, double, lavender-blue flowers; very fragrant.

Swanley White. Double white.

Russian. Very dark and fragrant.
15 cents each; ten for $1.50.

Grape-Dust is a Sure Cure for Mildew on Roses, etc.

RED ASTRACHAN APPLE.

Fruit Department.

☞ WRITE FOR SPECIAL PRICES on large quantities of any fruit trees.

Apples.

Prices.	Each.	Per 10.	Per 100.
Two years, 4 to 6 feet high	$0 25	$2 00	$15 00
One year, extra, 4 to 6 feet high	25	2 00	15 00
One year, extra, 3 to 4 feet high	25	1 50	12 00

Summer Varieties.

Benoni. Medium size, roundish, oblong, red ; flesh tender, juicy, rich ; valuable for the table.

Carolina June. Small or medium ; good and productive.

Early Harvest. Medium to large size ; pale yellow, with mild flavor ; a splendid apple for any purpose.

Early Strawberry. Medium size ; mostly covered with deep red ; tender, almost melting ; pleasant flavor.

Gravenstein. A very large, striped, roundish Apple, of the first quality.

Keswick Codlin. Large, oblong ; pale yellow ; pleasant acid ; of fair quality.

Maiden's Blush. Large, flat ; pale yellow, with a red cheek ; beautiful ; tender and pleasant, but not high-flavored.

Red Astrachan. Large, roundish, nearly covered with deep crimson, overspread with a thick bloom ; very handsome, juicy, good ; rather acid.

Sops of Wine. Medium size, oblong ; dark crimson flesh, stained with red ; sub-acid.

Sweet Bough. (Large Yellow Bough.) Large ; pale yellow ; sweet, tender and juicy.

Williams' Favorite. Large, oblong, red ; rich and excellent.

Our Collections of Flower Seeds (page 2 of the Cover) are Wonderfully Fine.

PEWAUKEE. (See page 80.)

Autumn Apples.

Alexander. Of Russian origin. A very large and beautiful deep red or crimson Apple of medium quality.

Arabskœ (Arabian Apple) Of Russian origin. Large, three inches in diameter; greenish yellow ground; flesh fine grained, white, juicy.

Fall Pippin. Very large, roundish, oblong, yellow; flesh tender, rich and delicious.

Fameuse (Snow Apple). Medium size; deep crimson; flesh snowy white, tender, melting and delicious.

Porter. Medium to large, oblong; yellow; flesh tender and of excellent flavor.

Golden Russet. Medium size, and russet, with a tinge of red on the exposed cheek.

Hubbardston's Nonesuch. Large; striped yellow and red; tender, juicy and fine.

Red Bietigheimer. A rare and valuable German variety; fruit very large, skin pale; cream colored ground, mostly covered with purplish crimson.

Roxbury Russet. Medium to large; surface rough, greenish, covered with russet; keeps till June.

Rhode Island Greening. Everywhere well-known and popular; fruit rather acid, but excellent for dessert and cooking.

Twenty Ounce. A very large, showy, striped Apple of fair quality.

Winter Varieties.

Baldwin. Large; bright red; crisp, juicy and rich; one of the most popular varieties for table use.

Belle de Boskoop. Large, bright yellow, washed with red on sunny side; flesh, crisp, firm, juicy; quality very good; a late keeper.

Ben Davis (New York Pippin, Kentucky Streak, etc.). A large, handsome, striped Apple of good quality.

Canada Reinette. Very large, flattened, ribbed; dull yellow; flesh firm, juicy and rich.

Cooper's Market (Cooper's Redling). Medium size, conical; red; handsome; quality good; one of the latest keepers and therefore very valuable.

Dominie (Wells of Ohio). A large, fine, striped apple, resembling the Rambo.

English Golden Russet. Medium size; dull russet, with a tinge of red on the sunny side; highly flavored.

Esopus Spitzenburg. Large; deep red, with gray spots, and densely covered with bloom; flesh yellow, crisp, rich and excellent.

Jonathan. Medium size; red and yellow; flesh tender, juicy and rich.

Lady Apple (*Pomme de Api*). A beautiful little dessert fruit; flat; pale yellow, with a bright red cheek; flesh crisp, juicy and pleasant.

Whale-Oil Soap is a cheap and effective Insecticide.

WHITNEY CRAB-APPLE.

Mann. Medium to large ; deep yellow, often with a shade of brownish red where exposed ; juicy, mild, pleasant, sub-acid.

Newtown Pippin (Yellow). Large ; firm, crisp, juicy, rich and highly flavored ; a great favorite in California, and is more extensively planted than any other variety.

Northern Spy. Large ; striped and covered on the sunny side with dark crimson, and coated with bloom.

Peck's Pleasant. Large ; pale yellow, with brown cheek ; very sweet and fair ; flesh firm and rich.

Pewaukee. (Origin Pewaukee, Wis.) Fruit medium to large ; skin of a bright yellow, striped and flashed with dark red.

Red Canada (Old Nonesuch, of Massachusetts). Medium size ; red, with white dots ; flesh rich, sub-acid and delicious.

Rome Beauty. Large ; yellow and bright red ; handsome ; medium quality.

Smith's Cider. Large, handsome ; red and yellow ; juicy, acid ; quality medium.

Swaar. Large ; pale lemon-yellow, with dark dots ; flesh tender, rich and spicy.

Talman's Sweeting. Medium size ; pale, whitish yellow, slightly tinged with red ; flesh firm, rich and sweet.

Vandevere (Newton Spitzenburg of the West). Medium size ; yellow, striped with red, and becoming deep crimson next the sun ; flesh yellow, rich and fine.

Wagner. Medium to large size ; deep red in the sun ; flesh firm, sub-acid and excellent.

Walbridge (Edgar Red-streak) Medium size ; skin pale yellow, shaded with red ; flesh crisp, tender, juicy.

Winesap. Large, roundish ; deep red ; medium quality ; keeps well.

York Imperial. Medium ; whitish, shaded with crimson in the sun ; firm, crisp, juicy, pleasant, sub-acid.

Yellow Bellflower. A fine, large, yellow Apple ; crisp and juicy flesh, and sprightly sub-acid flavor ; in use all winter ; very valuable.

Crab-Apples.

For Ornament or Preserving.

Hyslop. Very popular on account of its large size, beauty and hardiness ; very productive and a fine grower.

Paul's Imperial. Fairly large-sized fruit.

Red Siberian. Fruit small ; yellow, with scarlet cheek.

Van Wyck. Large ; handsome ; skin mottled with bright red ; sweet.

Whitney. Large, averaging one and a-half to two inches in diameter ; skin smooth, glossy green, striped and splashed with carmine ; juicy ; very pleasant.

Yellow Siberian (Golden Beauty). Large, and of a beautiful golden-yellow color.

WINDSOR CHERRY

Cherries.

	Each.	Per 10.	Per 100.
On Mazzard stocks, 2 years, 5 to 7 feet high	$0 35	$2 50	$18 00
" " " 1 year, 3 to 5 feet high	25	2 00	15 00

Hearts and Bigarreaus.

Belle d' Orleans. Above medium size ; roundish, heart-shaped ; whitish yellow, half covered with pale red ; very juicy, sweet and excellent. May to June.

Black Eagle. A very excellent English variety, ripening in June ; large size ; deep purple, or nearly black ; flesh deep purple, tender, with a rich, high-flavored juice.

Black Tartarian. Fruit of the largest size ; bright, purplish black ; flesh purplish, thick, juicy, very rich and delicious ; tree a remarkably vigorous, erect and beautiful grower, and an immense bearer ; the best of the black cherries.

Burr's Seedling. Large ; yellow, shaded with red ; sweet and rich ; vigorous and a great bearer.

Centennial. A seedling of Napoleon Bigarreau, raised by Mr. Harry Chapman, in Napa Valley, Cal. It is larger than its parent, more oblate in form, and beautifully marbled and splashed with crimson, on a pale yellow ground. Its sweetness is very marked. Its keeping qualities, after being taken from the tree, will undoubtedly render it the best cherry for shipment, specimens having been carried to the eastern states without apparent injury.

Cleveland Bigarreau. A thrifty, strong, spreading grower, and productive. Large ; clear red and yellow ; juicy, sweet and rich.

Coe's Transparent. Medium size ; pale amber, red and mottled next the sun ; tender, sweet and fine. Early June.

Early Purple Guigne. Small to medium size ; purple ; tender, juicy and sweet. May and June.

Early Rivers. A new early Cherry, of English origin. Tree luxuriant, healthy, and an abundant bearer ; fruit medium to large ; roundish heart-shaped ; skin deep black ; flesh very tender, sweet and agreeably perfumed ; stone very small.

Elton. Large, pointed ; pale yellow, nearly covered with light red ; juicy, with a very rich and luscious flavor ; one of the best.

Governor Wood. Large, light yellow, shaded with bright red ; flesh nearly tender, juicy, sweet, rich and delicious ; a vigorous grower and very productive.

Great Bigarreau (Monstreuse de Mezel). A foreign variety, of the largest size ; dark red or quite black ; firm and juicy ; late.

Knight's Early Back. Large ; black ; tender, juicy, rich and excellent ; high flavor.

Lewelling (Black Republican). A seedling raised by Seth Lewelling, of Oregon. Of large size ; supposed to be a cross between Napoleon Bigarreau and Black Tartarian, having the solid flesh of the former, and the color of the latter ; very late and good.

If you receive two Catalogues, give one to your neighbor.

EARLY RICHMOND CHERRY.

Lincoln. Large, pointed; brownish red when ripe; sprightly, juicy, pleasant; a very desirable sort.

Major Francis. A large, black, early Cherry, of fine flavor, and ripening before the Black Tartarian; tree vigorous and productive; one of the best early Cherries.

Napoleon Bigarreau (Royal Anne). A magnificent Cherry, of the largest size; pale yellow, becoming amber in the shade, richly dotted and spotted with deep red, and with a bright red cheek; flesh very firm, juicy and sweet; tree a free grower and an enormous bearer.

Pontiac. Large, dark purplish red; half tender, juicy and agreeable.

Rockport Bigarreau. Large; pale amber in the shade, light red in the sun; half tender, sweet and good; a very excellent and handsome Cherry; a good bearer.

Schmidt's Bigarreau. A new black Cherry, of the largest size; later than Great Bigarreau; very firm, and of excellent promise as a market and shipping variety.

Tendescant's Blackheart (Elkhorn). Large, heart-shaped; deep, glossy black; very solid and firm; dark purple; moderately juicy.

Werder's Early Black. An early variety, moderately productive; fruit large and excellent.

Willamette. A seedling from the Royal Anne, large, light red, sweet; tree an upright and vigorous grower.

Windsor. Originated with Mr. Jas. Dougall, Windsor, Canada, and sent out by Messrs. Ellwanger & Berry as a promising and valuable late variety for market and for family use. Fruit large; liver-colored, resembling the Elkhorn; flesh remarkably firm, and of fine quality.

Yellow Spanish. Large; pale yellow, with red cheek in the sun; flesh firm, juicy and delicious; one of the best, most beautiful and popular of all light-colored Cherries.

Dukes and Morellos.

	Each.	Per 10.	Per 100.
On Mazzard, 2 years, 5 to 7 feet high	$0 35	$2 50	$18 00
" " 1 year, 3 to 5 feet high	25	2 00	15 00

Belle Magnifique. A large, red, late Cherry; excellent for cooking, and fine for table when fully ripe; rather acid, tender, juicy and rich.

Duchesse de Palluau. Very large; oblate, and pitted apex; skin thin, of brilliant red color, becoming dark red as it ripens; flesh very tender and juicy, with a brisk and agreeable acidulous flavor.

Early Richmond. An early, red, acid Cherry; valuable for cooking early in the season.

Empress Eugenie. Large; dark red; flesh juicy, rich; similar in appearance and quality to the May Duke, ripening about ten days before it.

Our Menlo Park Lawn Grass (see page 2) is unsurpassed.

BARTLETT PEAR.

English Morello. Large; dark red, nearly black; tender, juicy, rich, acid; productive and late.

May Duke. An old, well-known variety; large; dark red; juicy, sub-acid, rich.

Nouvelle Royale. Fruit large, much more so than the May Duke; dark, glossy leaves and compact habit of growth; the largest and latest of the Duke Cherries

Olivet. The fruit is large, globular, very shining, deep red; the flesh is red, tender, rich and vinous, with a very sweet, sub-acidulous flavor. It continues to ripen for a period of six weeks, without losing its quality.

Reine Hortense. A French Cherry of great excellence; very large; finely mottled; tender, juicy, nearly sweet, and delicious.

Pears.

	Each.	Per 10.	Per 100.
On Pear stocks, 2 to 3 years, 5 to 7 feet high	$0 35	$2 50	$20 00
On Pear stocks, 1 year, 3 to 5 feet high	30	2 50	20 00
On Pear stocks, 1 year, Idaho and Zoe (new), 3 to 5 feet high . . .	75	5 00	40 00

Summer Varieties.

Andrew Desportes. Medium size; pale green, marbled on sunny side with red; flesh fine, juicy, melting.

Bartlett. One of the most popular pears; large, buttery and melting, with a rich, musky flavor.

Clapp's Favorite. A splendid Pear, resembling the Bartlett; ripens a few days earlier.

Dearborn's Seedling. Rather below medium size; pale yellow; melting and good.

Souvenir du Congress. Large to very large; we have had specimens which weighed 27 ounces, and which measured 24 inches in circumference; skin smooth; bright yellow when the fruit is fully matured; flesh, like Bartlett, is free from musky aroma; firm.

Summer. Doyenne (Doyenne d' Ete). A beautiful, melting, sweet Pear; rather small.

Tyson. Rather above medium size; melting, juicy, sweet and pleasant.

Our Collections of Seeds, Plants and Bulbs are of great value.

FLEMISH BEAUTY PEAR.

Select Autumn Pears.

Angouleme (Duchesse d' Angouleme). One of the largest of all our good Pears; as a dwarf it is one of the
most profitable market pears.
Belle Lucrative. Large, melting and sweet.
Bosc (Beurre Bosc). A large and beautiful russety Pear; very distinct, with a long neck; melting, or nearly so,
high flavored and delicious.
Boussock (Doyenne Boussock). A large Pear, of good quality.
Flemish Beauty. A large, beautiful, melting, sweet Pear.
Frederick Clapp. Size above medium; form generally obovate; skin thin, smooth, clear lemon-yellow; flesh
fine grained, very juicy and melting.
Hardy (Beurre Hardy). A large Pear; cinnamon-russet; melting and fine.
Kieffer (Kieffer's Hybrid). Said to have been raised from seed of the Chinese Sandbar. Large; skin rich,
golden yellow, sprinkled thickly with small dots, and often tinted with red on one side; juicy, melting.
Louise Bonne de Jersey. A large, beautiful, first-rate Pear; yellow, with a dark red cheek; melting, vinous,
buttery and rich.
Onondaga (Swan's Orange). A large, melting, sprightly, vinous Pear.
Seckel. The standard of excellence in the Pear; small, but of highest flavor.
Sheldon. A Pear of the very first quality; large, round; russet and red; melting, rich and delicious.
Urbaniste. A large, melting, buttery Pear, of first quality.

Select Winter Varieties.

Col. Wilder. Oblong, inclining to oval; skin yellow, profusely dotted and marbled with russet; flesh melting
and full of juice; sweet.
Dr. Reeder. Medium size; roundish ovate; skin yellow, netted with russet and sprinkled with russet dots.
Easter Beurre. A large, roundish oval fruit; yellow with a red cheek; melting and rich.
Josephine de Malines. Medium to large: roundish; pale straw color; flesh rose-colored; melting and
delicately perfumed; first quality.
Pound Pear. A monstrous fruit, and very beautiful; yellow with red cheek; for stewing.
P. Barry. Large; skin orange-yellow, covered with russet dots and blotches; flesh very juicy, buttery and
fine grained; flavor rich, excellent.

Have You tried our Menlo Park Pansies? You ought to!

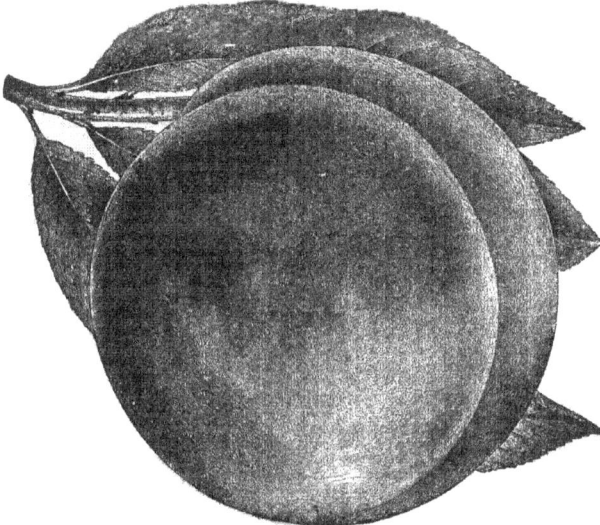

CRAWFORD'S EARLY PEACH.

Peaches.

	Each.	Per 10.	Per 100.
On Peach, 1 year, 3 to 5 feet high	$0 35	$3 50	$20 00

Alexander. Medium to large size; flesh melting, juicy, sweet; skin greenish white, covered with deep, rich red.

Amsden. Medium to large size; skin greenish white, nearly covered with purple in the sun; very good.

Coolidge's Favorite. A most beautiful and excellent Peach; skin white, delicately mottled with red; flesh pale; juicy and rich.

Crawford's Early. A magnificent, large, yellow Peach, of good quality.

Early York. Medium size; greenish white, covered in the sun with dull purplish red; rich and excellent.

Foster. Originated near Boston. A large, yellow Peach, resembling Crawford's Early, but of better quality.

George the Fourth. Large; white, with red cheek; flesh pale; juicy and rich.

Hale's Early. Raised in Ohio. Medium size; flesh white; first quality.

Large Early York. A large and beautiful variety; white, with a red cheek; flesh juicy and delicious.

Morris White. Medium size; dull, creamy white, tinged with red in the sun; flesh white to the stone; juicy and delicious.

Mountain Rose. Large, roundish; skin whitish, nearly covered with dark red; flesh white, juicy, very good.

Oldmixon Free. Large; greenish, white and red; flesh pale, juicy and rich.

Oldmixon Cling. Large and excellent; one of the best Clings.

Solway. An English Peach; large; roundish; skin creamy yellow; flesh deep yellow; juicy, melting, rich.

Susquehanna. A very large and superb yellow Peach from Pennsylvania; melting, rich and fine.

Ward's Late. A fine late Peach, resembling the Oldmixon.

Waterloo. Medium to large; round, with a deep suture on one side; skin pale, whitish green in the shade; juicy, vinous.

Wheatland. Large, roundish; skin golden yellow, shaded with crimson on the sunny side; flesh yellow, rather firm, juicy, sweet, and of fine quality.

Special prices will be quoted for large quantities.

WILD-GOOSE PLUM.

Plums.

	Each.	Per 10.	Per 100.
On Myrobolan, Clyman, 1 year, 4 to 6 feet high	$0 35	$3 00	$25 00
"　　　"　　　" 2 to 3 years, 4 to 6 feet high	35	3 00	25 00
"　　　"　　　" 1 year, 3 to 5 feet high	30	2 50	18 00

Bavay's Green Gage. One of the best foreign varieties; of fine flavor.
Bradshaw. A very large and fine red Plum; juicy and good; tree productive and a good grower.
Coe's Golden Drop. Large and handsome; light yellow; flesh rich and sweet, parting from the stone.
Duane's Purple. Very large and handsome; reddish purple; juicy and sweet; one of the very best.
General Hood. Very large; yellow, handsome; parts freely from stone.
Green Gage. Small, but of the highest excellence, and a general favorite.
Imperial Gage. Rather large; oval; greenish; juicy, rich and delicious.
Jefferson. A fine variety; yellow with a red cheek; flesh orange-colored.
Prince Engelbert. Very large and long; deep purple; rich and excellent; a standard variety in the east.
Quackenbos. Large; deep purple, covered with a dense blush bloom; flesh greenish, juicy; ranks good quality.
Smith's Orleans. A large and excellent variety; oval; reddish purple, with a thick coat of bloom; flesh yellow, juicy and rich.
Victoria (Shoop's Emperor). One of the most magnificent Plums in cultivation; of the largest size; fair quality; purplish red color.
Washington. A magnificent large Plum; roundish; green, usually marked with red; juicy, sweet and good.
Wild Goose (Native). A good variety of the Chickasaw; medium, roundish oblong, reddish yellow; juicy.
Yellow Gage. Rather large; yellow; oval; flesh yellow, juicy and rich.
Yellow Egg. A very large and beautiful egg-shaped yellow Plum; a little coarse, but excellent for cooking.

	Each.	Per 10.	Per 100.
Plum on Apricot, 1 year, 3 to 5 feet high	$0 25	$2 00	$15 00
"　　　"　　　" 2 years, 4 to 6 feet high	25	2 25	17 00

Varieties: Bavay's Green Gage, Jefferson, Kelsey Japan, Red Egg, Yellow Egg.

Prunes.

	Each.	Per 10.	Per 100.
On Myrobolan, 1 year, 3 to 5 feet high	$0 25	$2 00	$18 00
On Peach, 1 year, 3 to 5 feet high	35	3 00	25 00
On Apricot, 1 year, 3 to 5 feet high	25	2 00	15 00

Brignole. Medium, oblong; skin pale yellow, with a reddish cheek; flesh rich and sweet.
Bulgarian. Above medium size; dark purple; sweet and rich, with a pleasant acid flavor. An early bearer.

We will send ten varieties California Tree Seeds for One Dollar.

GERMAN PRUNE.

Datte de Hongrie (Hungarian Date Prune). Large, and very long fruit; skin dark purple, covered with a whitish bloom; flesh greenish yellow, firm, with a very rich flavor, resembling the German Prune; it parts freely from the stone, and makes a good drying Prune.

Fellenberg (Large German Prune, Swiss Prune, Italian Prune). Medium size, oval; dark purple; flesh juicy and delicious; parts from the stone; fine for drying; very productive.

French Prune (Petite d'Agen, Burgundy Prune). Extensively planted for drying; medium size, egg-shaped; violet-purple; juicy, very sweet, rich and sugary; prolific bearer.

German Prune (Common Quetsche). The fruit of the true German Prune is long, oval, and swollen to one side; skin purple, with a thick, blue bloom; flesh firm, green, sweet, with a peculiar, pleasant flavor; separates readily from the stone.

Golden Prune. Originated from the Italian Prune. Somewhat larger than its parent; of light golden color, exquisite flavor, and dries beautifully; the dried fruit averaging twenty-four to the pound; it is easily peeled, and separates readily from the stone, which is quite small for the size of the fruit; the tree is a beautiful grower, with heavy dark green foliage, and an abundant bearer.

Hungarian Prune (Grosse Prune, Pond's Seedling). Very large, dark red; juicy and sweet; its large size, bright color, productiveness and shipping qualities render it a profitable variety for home or distant market.

Robe de Sargent. Introduced from France. Fruit medium size, oval; skin deep purple, approaching to black, and covered with a thick blue bloom; flesh greenish yellow, sweet and well-flavored, sugary, rich and delicious, slightly adhering to the stone; a valuable drying and preserving variety.

Silver Prune. Said to be a seedling of Coe's Golden Drop, which it resembles. Fruit experts say it is entitled to rank with the best drying Plums and Prunes, because of its large size, handsome appearance and superior flavor.

St. Catherine. Medium size, narrowing considerably toward the stalk; skin very pale yellow, overspread with thin, white bloom; flesh yellow, juicy, rather firm, and adheres partially to the stone; flavor sprightly, rich and perfumed; a fine late variety.

St. Martin's Quetsche. A late variety from Germany; hardy and good bearer; fruit medium sized, ovate; skin pale yellow, covered with a violet bloom; flesh yellowish, with a rich and excellent flavor; separates readily from the stone.

Wangenheim. From Germany. Fruit medium size, oval; skin deep purple, covered with a thick blue bloom; flesh rather firm, greenish yellow, juicy, sugary, rich, and separates from the stone.

Tragedy Prune. A cross between the German Prune and Duane Purple. Fruit medium size; skin dark purple; flesh of yellowish green, very rich and sweet; frees readily from the pit; valuable for shipping.

Try a packet of our Perpetual-flowering Pelargoniums.

Grapes.

The vines listed below are raised in a locality where there is no phylloxera, and are perfectly healthy. We can furnish cuttings of any other varieties from vineyards free from phylloxera. Prices on application.

Table Grapes.

	Each.	10.	100.	1,000.
Muscat of Alexandria	$0 10	$0 75	$3 00	$20 00
Black Hamburg	10	75	3 00	20 00
Tokay	10	75	3 00	20 00
Rose of Peru	10	75	3 00	20 00
Black Morocco	10	75	3 00	20 00
Black Ferrara	10	75	3 00	20 00
Seedless Sultana	10	75	3 00	20 00
Emperor	10	75	3 00	20 00
Catawba	15	1 00		
Gros Blanc d' Espagne	15	1 00		
Black Muscat	15	1 00		
Delaware	15	1 00		
Almeria	15	1 00		
The Pierce (new)	50			

Red Wine.

	Each.	10.	100.	1,000.
Zingandel	10	75	3 00	20 00
Mataro	10	75	3 00	20 00
Carignon	10	75	3 00	20 00
Mondeuse	15	1 00	4 00	25 00
Cabernet Sauvignon	15	1 00	4 00	25 00
" Franc	15	1 00	4 00	25 00
Verdot	15	1 00	4 00	25 00
Petit Bouschet	15	1 00	4 00	25 00
" Pinot	15	1 00	4 00	25 00

White Wine.

	Each.	10.	100.	1,000.
Folle Blanche	10	75	3 00	20 00
Colombar	10	75	3 00	20 00
Semillon	15	1 00	4 00	25 00
Sauvignon Blanc	15	1 00	4 00	25 00
Muscadel du Bordelais	15	1 00	4 00	25 00

Resistant Vines.

	Each.	10.	100.	1,000.
Lenior	15	1 00	3 00	20 00
Riparia	15	1 00	3 00	20 00

APRICOTS.

OTHER FRUITS.

We include here a considerable list of other fruits, which are available for California growth, giving only a list of the varieties which are the best in each case.

APRICOT—

	Each.	Per 10.	Per 100
On Apricot. 1 year 3 to 5 feet	$0 30	$2 50	$20 00

Blenheim (Shipley), Early Moorpark, Hemskirke, Large Early Montgamet, Luizel, Moorpark, New Castle, Peach, Pringle, Royal.

On Peach. 1 year, 3 to 5 feet . . . . 30 · · 2 50 · 20 00
Blenheim (Shipley), Hemskirke, Moorpark, New Castle, Royal.

On Myrobolan. 1 year, 3 to 5 feet . . . . 30 · · 2 50 · 20 00
Blenheim, Hemskirke, Royal.

NECTARINE—

On Peach. 1 year, 3 to 5 feet . . . . 30 · 2 50 · 18 00
Boston, Downton, Early Newington, Elruge, Hardwick, Lord Napier, New White, Victoria.

QUINCE—

	Each.	Per 10.	Per 100
4 to 6 feet	35	2 50	18 00
3 to 4 feet	25	2 00	15 00

Apple (or Orange), Champion, Portugal, Rea's Mammoth.
Chinese and Meech's Prolific, 4 to 6 feet . . . . 50 · 4 00

FIG—

	Each.	Per 10.	Per 100
4 to 6 feet	35	2 50	20 00
3 to 4 feet	25	2 00	12 00
2 to 3 feet	20	1 50	10 00
1 to 2 feet	15	1 00	8 00

Black Ischia, Brown Turkey, Brunswick, Bulletin Smyrna, California Black, San Pedro, White Adriatic, White Genoa, White Ischia, White Marseilles.

	Each.	Per 10.	Per 100
New, 4 to 6 feet	50	4 00	
" 3 to 4 feet	40	3 50	
" 2 to 3 feet	35	3 00	

Agen, Angelique, Black Marseilles, Bondance Preoce, Bourjasotte Blanche, Bourjasotte Noir, Brown Ischia, Col. di Signora Bianca, Col. di Signora Nero, De Constantine, Du Roi, Early Violet, Grizzly Bourjasotte, Gros Grise Biferre, Grossale, Hirta du Japan, Ladaro, Monaco Bianco, Negro Largo, Osborn's Prolific, Pastiliere, Rocardi, Ronde Violet Native, Royal Vineyard, Yellow Celestial.

Our Collections of Plants and Bulbs are of great value.

AMERICAN SWEET CHESTNUT.

	Each.	Per 10.	Per 100
ALMOND—			
On Almonds. 1 year, 3 to 5 feet	$0 30	$2 50	$20 00
" 1 year. 2 to 3 feet	25	2 00	18 00
Drake's Seedling, Flat-fruited or Hard-shell, Marie Dupuys, Ne Plus Ultra, Non-pareil, IXL, King's Soft-shell, Languedoc, Paper-shell, Pistache, Sultana.			
BUTTERNUT—			
5 to 7 feet	1 00	7 50	
3 to 4 feet	75	5 00	
2 to 3 feet	50	3 50	
CHESTNUT—			
American Sweet, 2 to 3 feet	50	4 00	
Italian or Spanish, 6 to 8 feet	75	5 00	40 00
" " 4 to 6 feet	50	4 00	35 00
" " 3 to 4 feet	35	3 00	25 00
" " 2 to 3 feet	30	2 00	20 00
Japan Mammoth (grafted), 3 to 4 feet	75	5 00	
Maron Combale, Maron de Lyon and Numbo (grafted). 4 to 6 feet	75	5 00	
" " " " " 3 to 4 feet	50	4 00	
" " " " " 2 to 3 feet	40	3 50	
Maron de Lyon (grafted). 8 to 10 feet	50	10 00	
" " 6 to 8 feet	1 00	7 50	
FILBERTS—			
English Red Hazel 3 to 4 feet	75	5 00	
" " 2 to 3 feet	50	4 00	
Named Sorts. 4 to 6 feet	1 00	7 50	
Cosford Nut, Dwarf Prolific, Imp. de Trebizond, Macrocarpa, Mer. de Bollivillar, Nottingham.			
PECAN—			
4 to 5 feet	50	4 00	
3 to 4 feet	40	3 50	
2 to 3 feet	35	3 00	
PISTACHIO NUT—			
3 to 5 feet	1 00	7 50	
WALNUT—			
American Black, transplanted, 10 to 12 feet	1 00	7 50	
" " " 8 to 10 feet	75	5 00	
" " " 6 to 8 feet	50	4 00	30 00
" " " 4 to 6 feet	35	3 00	25 00
" " " 3 to 4 feet	30	2 50	20 00
California " " 10 to 12 feet	1 00	7 50	
" " " 8 to 10 feet	50	4 00	30 00
" " " 6 to 8 feet	35	3 00	25 00

We can guarantee satisfaction, because we know what we sell.

LOQUAT.

	Each.	Per 10.	Per 100.
WALNUTS, Continued—			
English, transplanted, 8 to 10 feet	$0 75	$5 00	
" 6 to 8 feet	50	4 00	$30 00
" 4 to 6 feet	40	3 00	20 00
" 3 to 4 feet	30	2 50	18 00
" 2 to 3 feet	25	2 00	15 20
A Bijou, transplanted, 2 to 3 feet	50	4 00	
Chaberte, Franquette, Vourey (grafted on English). 8 to 10 feet	1 00	7 50	
ORANGE—			
Florida grown, on sour stocks, naked roots, 3 to 4 feet	1 25	10 00	90 00
Maltese Blood, Mediterranean Sweet, Washington Navel.			
LEMON—			
Florida grown, on Sour stocks, naked roots, 3 to 4 feet	1 25	10 00	90 00
Eureka, Villa Franca.			
PERSIMMON—			
Japanese (grafted, grown here), 2 years, 3 to 4 feet	50	4 00	30 00
Japanese (imported), 1 year, 3 to 4 feet	35	2 50	20 00
American, 6 to 8 feet	75	5 00	
" 4 to 6 feet	50	4 00	
POMEGRANATE—			
Sweet-fruited and Sub-acid, 2 to 3 feet	35	2 50	
Sweet-fruited and Sub-acid, 3 to 4 feet	50	4 00	
Sweet-fruited, 3 to 4 feet	50	4 00	
Paper-shell and Ruby, 2 to 3 feet	75	5 00	
GUAVA—			
Pot-grown, 1½ to 2 feet	50	4 00	
" 1 to 1½ feet	40	3 50	
CAROB—			
Pot-grown, 1½ to 2 feet	1 00	7 50	
HOVENIA—			
Dulcis (pot-grown), 3 to 4 feet	1 00	7 50	
" (pot-grown), 2 to 3 feet	75	5 00	
LOQUAT—			
Large-fruited (grafted), 1 to 2 feet	75	6 00	
Seedlings, 3 to 4 feet	60	5 00	
" 2 to 3 feet	50	4 00	
" Pot-grown, 1 to 1½ feet	50	4 00	
MEDLAR—			
Nottingham, 2 to 3 feet	75		
MULBERRY—			
Downing, Lick's, New American and Russian, 8 to 10 feet	50	4 00	30 00
" " 5 to 7 feet	35	3 00	25 00
Persian (trans.), 4 to 6 feet	50	4 00	
" " 2 to 3 feet	35	3 00	

One trial will convince you that "QUALITY" is our motto.

PICHOLINE OLIVE.

OLIVE—

	Each.	Per 10.	Per 100.
Mission, 6 to 8 feet	$0 75	$6 00	$45 00
" 4 to 5 feet	60	5 00	40 00
" 3 to 4 feet	50	4 00	30 00
Picholine, 3 to 4 feet	40	3 00	20 00
" 2 to 3 feet	35	2 00	15 00
" 1 to 2 feet	25	1 50	12 00
" (Grafted), 6 to 8 feet	1 50	10 00	75 00
" " 4 to 6 feet	1 00	7 50	60 00
" " 3 to 4 feet	75	6 00	50 00
" " 2 to 3 feet	60	5 00	40 00
Amellau, Atro-rubens, Atro-violacea, Nevadillo Blanco, Oblonga, Polymorpha.			

GOOSEBERRY—

	Each.	Per 10.	Per 100.
English, Whinham's Industry, 1 year	40	3 50	
" Assorted, 2 years	35	3 00	25 00
" " 1 year	30	2 50	20 00
Houghton, 2 years	25	1 50	7 50
" 1 year	20	1 00	6 00
Smith's Imp., 1 year	25	1 50	7 50

BLACKBERRY—

	Each.	Per 10.	Per 100.
Crandall's Early, Dorchester, Kittatinny and Lawton		50	2 50
Ancient Briton, Snyder, Early Harvest, Evergreen and Wilson Early	15	1 00	5 00
Wilson, Jr. and Erie	35	2 00	15 00

DEWBERRY—

	Each.	Per 10.	Per 100.
Lucretia	15	1 00	7 50

RASPBERRY—

	Each.	Per 10.	Per 100.
Red varieties : Cuthbert, Lost Rubies, Hansell, Herstine		50	2 00
" " Falstolf, Franconia, Marlboro, Reliance		1 00	3 00
Yellow varieties : Caroline, Golden Queen, Yellow Antwerp	20	1 50	5 00
Black Caps : Davidson's Thornless, Doolittle, Gregg, Hilbourne, Mammoth Cluster, Ohio, Schaffer's Colossal, Tyler		1 00	5 00

STRAWBERRY—

	Each.	Per 10.	Per 100.
Captain Jack, Jersey Queen, Longworth's Prolific, Miner's Prolific, Wm. Parry, Sharpless, Wilson's Albany		50	2 00
Bomba, Bubach's No. 5, Gandy, Jessie, May King, Ontario, Pearl		75	3 00
Eureka, Felton, Lovett's Early, Michel's Early, Parker Earle, Schuster's Gem		1 00	4 00

Order now; don't wait until you are going to plant.

CUTHBERT RASPBERRY   (See page 92.)

	Each.	Per doz.	Per 100.
ARTICHOKE—			
Green Globe, 2 year old roots	$0 20	$2 00	
ASPARAGUS—			
Conover's Colossal, 2 year old roots . . . . per 1000, $10 00			$2 00
Palmetto (new), 2 year "			2 25
HOP ROOTS		50	
HORSE-RADISH		50	
RHUBARB—			
Myatt's Linnæus	25	1 50	12 00
Lorenzo	50	3 00	
TARRAGON ROOTS	25	2 50	

RHUBARB.

Public Institutions requiring large quantities supplied on special terms.

Agricultural and Horticultural Books.

Any of the following publications will be sent by mail or express, prepaid, on receipt of price, and we will endeavor to find for our patrons any publications pertaining to horticulture or kindred subjects, which will be supplied at publisher's price.

The Illustrated Dictionary of Gardening. A practical Encyclopedia of Horticulture for Gardeners and Botanists. By G. Nicholson, and others. *Illustrated with numerous full-page plates printed in colors, and over 2,000 accurately executed wood-cuts in the text.* The most complete work of the kind published, giving full particulars regarding all kinds of exotic and hardy plants and vegetables cultivated. 4 vols., imp. 8vo, including the supplement of new species and varieties, cloth, gilt edges, $20.

Henderson's New Hand-Book of Plants and General Horticulture. A dictionary of the principal cultivated plants, with short descriptions, and an extensive glossary of botanical and horticultural terms. 1 vol., imp. 8vo, cloth, $4.

Mushrooms : How to Grow Them. A practical treatise on Mushroom Culture for Profit and Pleasure. By Wm. Falconer. Cloth, 12mo, $1.50.

Practical Floriculture. A Guide to the Successful Propagation and Cultivation of Florists' Plants. By Peter Henderson. New enlarged edition. *With numerous Illustrations.* 12mo, cloth, $1.50.

How Crops Grow. A Treatise on the Chemical Composition, Structure and Life of the Plant. By Prof. Samuel W. Johnson, of Yale College. New edition, entirely rewritten and greatly enlarged. *With numerous Illustrations.* 12mo, cloth, $2.

How Crops Feed. By Prof. Samuel W. Johnson. A Treatise on the Atmosphere and the Soil as Relating to the Nutrition of Agricultural Plants. *With Illustrations.* 12mo, cloth, $2.

Gardening for Pleasure. A Guide to the Amateur in the Fruit, Vegetable and Flower Garden, with full Directions for the Greenhouse and Window Garden. By Peter Henderson. *With Illustrations.* 12mo, cloth, $2.

Gardening for Profit. A Guide to the Successful Culture of the Market and Family Garden. *With numerous Illustrations.* By Peter Henderson. New edition, entirely rewritten and greatly enlarged. 12mo, cloth, $2.

The Tuberous Begonia, its History and Cultivation. With a Select List of Varieties. 12mo, paper, 50 cents.

Grasses and Forage Plants. A Practical Treatise on Fodder Plants in the United States and British Provinces. By Chas. L. Flint. Revised edition. $2.

Practical Forestry. A Treatise on the Propagation, Planting and Cultivation, with Descriptions, of the Indigenous Trees of the United States. With notes on a large number of valuable exotic species. By A. S. Fuller. *Illustrated.* 12mo, cloth, $1.50.

The Nursery Book. A Complete Hand-book of Propagation and Pollination. By Prof. L. H. Bailey, of the Cornell Experiment Station. The book tells plainly and briefly what every one who sows a seed, makes a cutting or sets a graft wants to know. *With about 100 Illustrations.* 12mo, cloth, $1.

The Horticulturist's Rule-Book. By L. H. Bailey. Contains a great number of rules and receipts used by Florists, Gardeners, Farmers, etc., etc. Revised edition. 12mo, cloth, $1.

Truck Farming at the South. A Guide for the Raising of Vegetables for the Markets. By Dr. A. Oemler. Gives full cultural directions; also, methods of packing. $1.50.

Asparagus Culture. An account of the best methods employed in England and France ; alike useful to the amateur and professional gardener. By Wm. Robinson. 50 cents.

The New Potato Culture. By Elbert S. Carman. This book gives the results of 15 years' experimental work on the Rural grounds, and treats of new and profitable methods. *With Illustrations.* Price, cloth, 75 cents ; paper, 40 cents.

Spraying Crops : Why, When and How to Do It By Prof. Clerance M. Weed. A handy volume of about 100 pages. *Illustrated.* Covers the whole field of the insect and fungous enemies of crops for which the spray is used. Price, stiff paper cover, 50 cts,; flexible cloth, 75 cts.

First Lessons in Agriculture. (Second Edition, Revised and Enlarged.) By F. A. Gulley, M. S., of the Mississippi Agricultural College. This book discusses the more important branches of science related to agriculture, supplies a much-needed text-book for common-schools, and is useful for the practical farmer. It includes all the latest developments in agricultural science as applied to the subject. Price, cloth, $1. Special prices for schools and colleges.

Fruit Culture, and the Laying Out and Management of a Country Home. By W. C. Strong. A new and revised edition, with many additions, making it the latest and freshest book on the subject. *Illustrated.* Price, in one volume, 16mo, cloth, $1.

Useful Tables for Planters, Farmers and Gardeners.

Quantity of Seed Required to Sow an Acre of Ground.

	Pounds to Acre.		Pounds to Acre.
Alfalfa or Lucerne	25 to 30	Grass, Mesquite (in the chaff)	35
Asparagus	5	" Hungarian	25
Barley—Broadcast	125 to 150	" Millet, German	25
Beans, Dwarf or Bush—Hills	40	" Menlo Park Lawn Mixture	60
Beans, Dwarf or Bush—Drills	80	" Johnson Grass or Evergreen Millet	25 to 30
Beans, Tall or Pole—Hills	25	Hemp—Broadcast	40 to 50
Beet—Garden	10	Melon, Water—Hills	2 to 3
Beet—Field	8	Melon, Musk—Hills	2
Broom Corn—Drills	12	Oats—Broadcast	80
Buckwheat—Broadcast	35	Onion Seed, in Drills	5
Cabbage, in beds, to cover an acre after		" Sets, in Drills	250
transplanting	½	" Seed, for Sets	30 to 40
Carrot—Drills	3	Parsnip, in Drills	5
Clover, Red alone—Broadcast	10	Peas, in Drills	100
Clover, White alone—Broadcast	8	Peas—Broadcast	200
Clover, Alsike—Broadcast	6	Potatoes, in Hills	500 to 600
Corn, Sweet or Field—Hills	15	Pumpkin, in Hills	8
Corn, to cut green for fodder—Drilled or		Radish, in Drills	8
Broadcast	125	Rye—Broadcast	100
Cucumber—Hills	2	Spinach, in Drills	10
Flax (when wanted for seed)	30	Squash, Bush varieties, in Hills	4
Flax (when wanted for fiber)	50	Squash, Running varieties, in Hills	3
Grass, Kentucky Blue (for pasture)	45	Tomato—In beds to transplant	½
" Kentucky Blue (for lawns)	60 to 80	Turnip and Ruta-Baga—Drills	2
" Orchard	40	Turnip and Ruta-Baga—Broadcast	3
" English Rye	30	Vetches—Broadcast	150
" Italian Rye	30 to 40	Wheat—Broadcast	100
" Red Top	30	Wheat, in Drills	75
" Timothy	20		

Number of Trees, Plants, etc., required to set an acre at given distances.

Distance apart each way.	No. of plants.	Distance apart each way.	No. of plants.
1 foot	43,560	12 feet	302
2 "	10,890	14 "	222
3 "	4,840	15 "	193
4 "	2,722	16 "	176
5 "	1,742	18 "	134
6 "	1,210	20 "	108
7 "	888	25 "	69
8 "	680	30 "	48
9 "	537	35 "	33
10 "	435	40 "	27

Average Profitable Longevity of Fruit-Plants under High Culture.

Apples	25 to 40 years.	Pear	50 to 75 years.
Blackberry	8 to 12 "	Persimmon, or Kaki, as long as an apple tree.	
Currant	20 "	Plum	20 to 25 years.
Gooseberry	20 "	Raspberry	8 to 12 "
Orange and Lemon	50 or more.	Strawberry	3 "
Peach	8 to 12 years.		

Average Distances for Planting.

	Distance apart each way.		Distance apart each way.
Apples—Standard	30 to 40 feet.	Peaches	16 to 18 feet
" Pyramidal	15 to 18 "	Apricots	16 to 18 "
" Dwarf (bushes)	10 "	Nectarines	16 to 18 "
Pears—Standard	20 to 25 "	Quinces	10 to 12 "
" Pyramidal	16 to 18 "	Currants	3 to 4 "
" Dwarf	10 "	Gooseberries	3 to 4 "
Cherries—Standard	18 to 20 "	Raspberries	3 to 4 "
" Dukes and Morellos	16 to 18 "	Blackberries	6 to 7 "
Plums—Standard	16 to 18 "	Strawberries	1½ to 3 "
" Pyramidal	10 to 14 "		

A Rule to Find the Number of Plants Required for an Acre.

Multiply the width by the breadth, in feet, and see how many times the number is contained in 43,560, the number of square feet in an acre. For instance, plants set 2x3 feet, each plant would require six square feet—43,560 divided by 6 gives 7,260—the number of plants required for an acre at the above distances.

INDEX.

J. HORACE McFARLAND CO., HORTICULTURAL PRINTERS, HARRISBURG, PA.

BEAUTIFUL NEW CANNAS

* * * * * * *

F EW FLOWERING plants combine so many qualities of excellence as the modern race of Cannas. They are ornamental, whether in your hothouse or on your veranda, in your garden, or grown in a clump on your lawn. In luxuriance of foliage and gracefulness of bloom the Canna is queen. We do not present an engraving, as we would like, because it seems impossible to do justice to the Canna. The versatile florists' artist, Mr. Blanc, assures us that he has never yet made a successful Canna picture, and believes the glowing colors and rich foliage cannot be adequately presented in black and white. Following our determination to be leading in every feature, one of our managers on a recent tour took especial pains to obtain the best selections of Cannas now before the world. He inspected each of the varieties so far produced, and we are thus qualified to save you the annoying trouble of experiment, by offering only such Cannas as you yourself would likely have chosen. In selecting, we gave due consideration to height, colors of foliage and flowers, as well as freeness of growing, and we can emphatically say that what we now offer are the choicest collections obtainable. They are :

Best Dozen Standard Varieties.

These give a wide range in color of flowers and foliage; and the twelve splendid Cannas may be arranged in a most effective manner planted together.

MAD. CROZY. Undoubtedly the finest and most distinct variety yet introduced. The flowers are of the largest size, of a dazzling crimson-scarlet color, bordered with golden yellow; the plant is of vigorous growth, yet dwarf in habit, seldom exceeding four feet in height; the foliage is of a rich, cheerful green and very massive; the flowers are produced in large branching stems, which are closely set with bloom, each stem being really a bouquet in itself.

MR. LEFEBVRE. Flowers of large size, of a rich carmine; foliage bronzy purple; 4½ feet.

MLLE. DE CRUILLON. Flowers of large size, of a light yellow, shading to terra-cotta in the center; a distinct and attractive variety; foliage light green; 3½ feet.

PRESIDENT HARDY. Flowers pure salmon on a light yellow ground; very attractive; foliage green; 4½ feet.

SECRETAIRE NICHOLAS. Flowers rich salmon-red, overlaid with orange; of large size; foliage pea-green; 3½ feet.

PRESIDENT CARNOT. Deep purple foliage; flowers of good size, reddish crimson; 5 feet.

GEOFFREY ST. HILLAIRE. Flowers large orange, overlaid with scarlet; very distinct; foliage bronzy purple; 5 feet.

ENFANT DU RHONE. Very floriferous; flowers of good size; bright salmon, splashed with cinnabar-red and orange-scarlet; very distinct; foliage dark green; 3½ feet.

FRANCOIS CROZY. Bright apricot, shaded orange, distinctly edged with golden yellow; foliage dark green; 3 feet.

INGENIEUR ALPHAND. Flowers reddish carmine, overlaid with crimson; of large size; foliage bronzy purple; 5 feet.

PRINCESS DE BRANCOVEN. Flowers of medium size, of an orange-brown color, edged with gold; foliage green; 4½ feet.

DUCHESS DE MONTENARD. Very large flowers of a rich, bright yellow, spotted with red; foliage green; 4½ feet.

Price, 30 cents each, or $3 for the entire collection.

The Newest and Choice Cannas.

The French growers are always improving their productions, and the five varieties below are the best they have sent out to date. Of course, they are scarce as yet, and consequently high in price; but their merit will make them welcome.

ALPHONSE BOUVIER. This is a perfect gem among the bright colored varieties, being the most intensely brilliant crimson yet introduced, and is undoubtedly the best bedding variety for planting in masses now in cultivation; on first opening the flowers are of an intensely brilliant crimson, approaching scarlet, changing to a deep crimson as they fully develop; the foliage is of a rich green; the plant is of strong, robust habit and exceedingly floriferous—thus it is likely to be one of the best for bedding; 5 feet.

PAUL MARQUANT. An exceedingly distinct and novel variety, being entirely different from all others; its flowers, which are of immense size, are borne in stiff, upright, branching heads, and are of a peculiar salmon-scarlet color, which passes to a rosy carmine as they fully develop; the plant is of dwarf habit, rarely exceeding 3½ feet; foliage bright green. Thus the variety is thoroughly unique in character and should be of great value, even for pot culture.

J. D. CABOS. Another distinct variety, with large, orange colored flowers, overlaid with a bright tinge of scarlet; the foliage, which is of a heavy bold appearance, is of rich bronzy purple; height 5 feet.

CAPITAINE P. SUZZONI. The best yellow yet introduced. The ground color is of a rich canary-yellow, with broad, heavy petals, the entire flower being spotted with small dots of cinnamon-red; foliage light green; 4 feet.

GUSTAVE SENNHOLZ. A most peculiar and distinct variety, producing its flowers in close, upright trusses, reminding one of a stem of Gladiolus; in color they are of a distinct shade of rosy salmon, changing to a very light shade of the same color as the flowers fully develop; the foliage is of a light green color, edged with purple; grows 3½ feet high. On account of its entirely distinct appearance we believe this variety will become a great favorite.

Price, $1.25 each, or $5 for the Collection.

SPRING DELIVERY. BOOK YOUR ORDERS NOW.

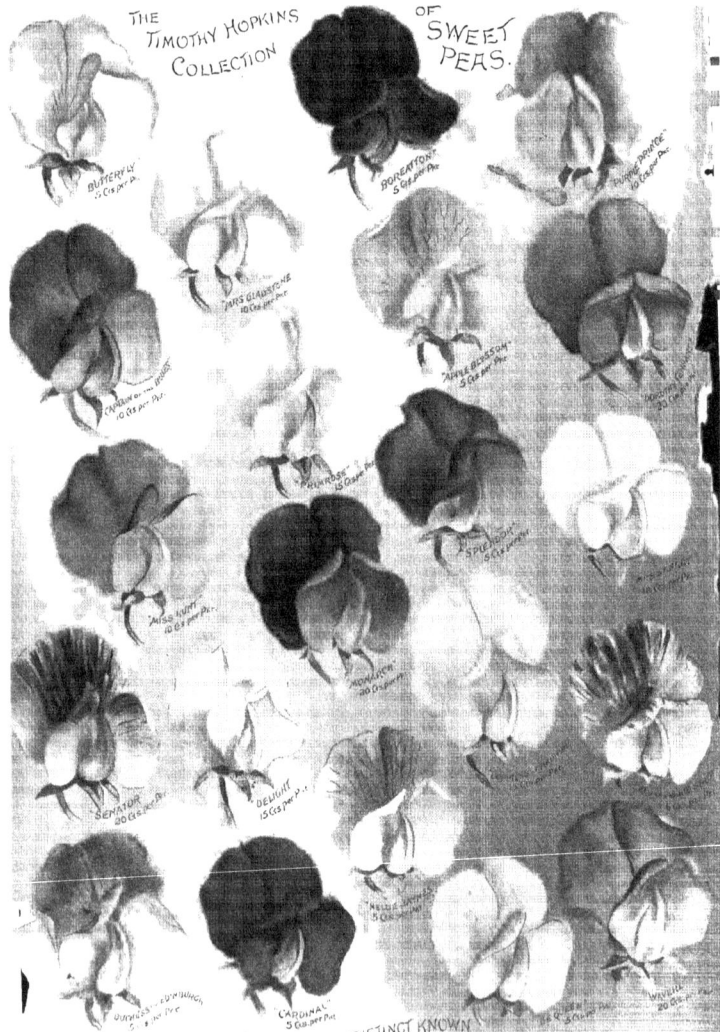

THE TIMOTHY HOPKINS COLLECTION OF SWEET PEAS.

THESE 21 VARIETIES. THE MOST DISTINCT KNOWN FOR $1.50

www.ingramcontent.com/pod-product-compliance
Lightning Source LLC
Chambersburg PA
CBHW031443280326
41927CB00038B/1596